W9-BFA-240

LYNNE BUNDESEN

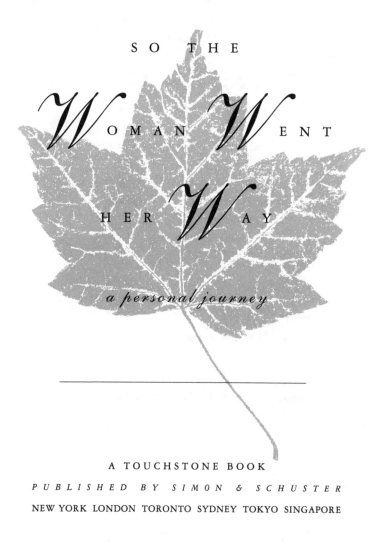

SO THE

WOMAN WENT

HER WAY

a personal journey

A TOUCHSTONE BOOK

PUBLISHED BY SIMON & SCHUSTER

NEW YORK LONDON TORONTO SYDNEY TOKYO SINGAPORE

SIMON & SCHUSTER/TOUCHSTONE

Simon & Schuster Building
Rockefeller Center
1230 Avenue of the Americas
New York, New York 10020

Designed by Pei Loi Koay
Manufactured in the United States of America

10 9 8 7 6 5 4 3 2 1
10 9 8 7 6 5 4 3 2 1 *(Pbk)*

Library of Congress Cataloging-in-Publication Data

Bundesen, Lynne
    So the woman went her way : a personal journey / Lynne
    Bundesen.
        p.   cm.
    "A Touchstone book."
    1. Bundesen, Lynne. 2. Christian biography—United States
    3. Women—Religious life. 4. Women in the Bible. I. Title.
    BR1725.B75A3   1993
    248.8'43—dc20

                                    92-34758
                                    CIP

ISBN 0-671-67701-2
0-671-67702-0 *(pbk)*

CONTENTS

PART   FOUR

Thomas Arthur Bundesen

1960–1990

$\mathcal{I}$NTRODUCTION

THERE IS NO ONE who is not on a journey. And, whether the journey is in unbroken lines or zigs and zags, it is individual. The journey described in this book took place on several continents, over several decades. It is neither the full story of a life nor of the times. It is a partial description of encounters that I have had with the women, men and children of the Bible. Some of these encounters have been with self-described, literal, "born-again, evangelical, Bible-believing Christians." Others still have been with men and women who say they don't believe a word of the Original Text.

Some of the encounters have been with the Word of the Book alone. These are the encounters that have changed my perspective and that set me off across the earth in search of the only God that I, as a woman born in the United States between the Depression and the War, could know. The God of Abraham, Isaac, Jacob and Paul.

I have come to know this God as also the God of Sarah, Rebekah, Rachel and Mary Magdalene. And, I am learning more about myself and this God in the process.

—Lynne Bundesen

$\mathscr{P}$ R O L O G U E

I WOULD LIKE to live in a spiritually perfect universe. Instead, I am at a dinner just outside Santa Fe. There are twelve of us in the room. Two men are sitting by the fire. They are in the middle of a seven-day fast and prefer not to sit at the table with the rest of us. A woman who has just begun a sexual liaison with one of them pulls her chair between the men.

Loud enough for all of us to hear, she says, "You know, there are secret manuscripts in a monastery in Lhasa that tell how Jesus really treated women."

"And how is that?" I ask.

She stares at me as if she didn't understand.

Thinking perhaps she really doesn't know how Jesus treated women, I say, "You don't have to go all the way to Tibet to find that out. It's in the Bible. I've got one here, in my purse, if you want to take a look."

She looks at me, forehead crinkled, as if to say, "The Bible? Don't you know better?"

I am surprised. The woman is not interested in information that might be within reach. It is written all over her body, in the darkening of her eyes, the flush rising on her cheeks, the way her shoulders shift and arms wave off a suggestion that knowledge of how Jesus treated women might be at hand.

What does interest her is the gap between how her new love is viewing her and how she wants to be seen. What obsesses her is her current self. She is draped over a chair crying out for attention and respect that she somehow senses are not really here for her tonight but that she hopes exist in hidden documents in a far-off place guarded by strange men from another culture and a distant past.

If I told her that I was a Celtic princess descended from the Valkyrie and that my sisters, the trees, talked to me about the healing of men and nations, she would believe me. But if I told her the Bible was about her life, she would think I was selling a doctrine.

I want to tell her to take a pass on this parody by the fireplace, leave the men alone, go to bed, relax, find refuge in the everlasting arms, let the wings of God nourish her in sleep. But as a guest I remain silent and ponder. How the Word treats women is one of the best-kept secrets of all time. Perhaps she believes the heartbreaking lie of the ages—that the Bible is a book about an absent and sexist God who lets men treat women badly with His approval.

Yet, within its pages rests securely a narrative of spiritual power for women. From Genesis to Revelation, from the fatal attraction between Adam and Eve to the bliss of the new heaven and new earth, the Bible is a sea of glass in which to view the sacred, female self.

The woman renting the estate where the meal is being served refers to herself as the steward of the property. She informs me that she is "channeling the Magdalene."

In just three words my hostess has made a surreal connection between a cultural phenomenon and one of the most far-sighted and least understood women in the Judeo-Christian culture. The candles flicker and the glow from their flame spreads across the table. The breeze from the mountains, full of juniper and pinon, enters the room like a waving flag.

My hostess claims to know what the first person to see the risen Christ saw, heard, felt, knew. I ask her if she is writing down the messages that are coming to her from the only person understood by all four gospels to have been an eyewitness to the Resurrection.

"I don't have to," she says. "I have money. I'm spending my time developing television shows on socially conscious investments."

I hear a small sound, a pop, in my ear. Channeling the

Magdalene passed up for socially conscious investments?

The food is served and we all join hands and make the sound of "Om." There are squeezes on both my hands from people who have never met me before. French phrases are dropped into the conversation, and Velveeta cheese is served melted over the shrimp. I've always thought you could judge people's religious attitude by the food they eat. The conversation resembles the food. There is no common issue nor topic in the air, no thought nor idea nor speculation that can sustain itself long enough to find form.

After dinner the hostess goes to the kitchen to roll a cigarette. I join her at the kitchen table, hoping she will develop the idea of channeling the Magdalene and at the same time give me some insight into herself. I am heartened that she senses Mary Magdalene might have something to say to women today and I feel we are finally communicating until she says, "I go to Hawaii a lot. I really find inner space there."

"I thought people came to Santa Fe for that reason," I say.

As an afterthought to inner space in Hawaii she responds, "Those manuscripts in Ladakh are something I want to read."

Ladakh? Lhasa? Each to her own.

"There is an awful lot of Magdalene energy in the south

of France," she continues in a matter-of-fact voice. "You know, don't you, that Mary Magdalene went to the south of France after Jesus' crucifixion—taking their child?"

I have no idea what Magdalene energy is, but I have an open mind. An eyewitness account of Jesus' life and ministry in the words of Mary Magdalene would put this dinner over the top, serve my soul and body better than the Om and the shrimp, the coffee and cigarettes. I'd like to know how Mary felt when the men didn't believe her report of the Resurrection.

Now when Jesus was risen early the first day of the week, he appeared first to Mary Magdalene, out of whom he had cast seven devils. And she went and told them that had been with him, as they mourned and wept. And they, when they had heard that he was alive, and had been seen of her, believed not, says Mark in his gospel account.

And their words, says Luke, who has reports from several other women at the scene, *seemed to them as idle tales and they believed them not.*

Did Mary feel rejected when the men discounted her report? Or did she go her way, comforted in what she had seen and heard?

"It is hard work being a channel for Mary Magdalene," says my hostess as she takes the last puff of her smoke.

"I had a vision recently of a cosmic egg, and man and

---

woman were inside the shell. It's a very powerful idea and I feel responsible for getting this information out somehow, but it's not really my work," she says with a sigh.

Reaching into my image bank, groping for common ground, I say tentatively, "I lived for a while in the Philippines. The Filipino Creation story has male and female created simultaneously out of water. Do you think that is a spin on the first chapter of Genesis where God creates male and female simultaneously?"

Silently she contemplates her vision, as she crushes out her cigarette.

We are not speaking the same language. Her image bank is *2001, A Space Odyssey.* Here we are at a table on the edge of the millennium. She swears that but for socially conscious investments she would be channeling the Magdalene full time. On the other side of the table, I am convinced that Mary of Magdala is the woman who reported the biggest news story of all time.

We live in parallel universes. Can my hostess hear her own voice? Does she long so to be some undefined other place that she cannot enjoy the breeze and the coffee much less the quiet of the night? What ever happened to conversation?

Dinner is over. It is time for the sweat, an Indian tradition. A fire has been burning outside during dinner, and rocks have been collecting heat. We walk down the hill, joined by two small children who have been fed in another part of the house, leaving the lights of the house for the light of the fire.

A woman strips to enter the tent where the sweat is taking place. Except for the tent it looks to me like the saunas and Finn baths that I took as a child with my family in northern Minnesota.

A child starts to cry, and some of the adults tell him to be quiet. I can tell that the four-year-old does not understand why his mother is going with no clothes on into a tent with six other naked men and women.

I have not yet disrobed and, taking him by the hand, suggest we look for a cookie in the house as I wait my turn for the sweat. We walk up the hill, and he shows me the way to go to find the kitchen. We search through cabinet after cabinet. Wheat germ, noodles, dried tomatoes, nuts. Not an Oreo or a Mallomar, not a Milano in sight.

"What kind of house is it," I say, "without a cookie?"

"Not a very good house," he says.

Are there no cookies in the New Age?

We go back down the hill to the fire and the people in the tent and the two couples who are caressing each other and the others who are sitting and waiting their turn to enter the sweat. The hostess comes out of the tent where she has been with the other guests calling on the power of the hot rocks, asking to forgive their parents for past sins, channeling energy from the Divine Mother and the Universe.

It is a question of style, I tell myself. What is authentic to American Indians looks peculiar when practiced by these transplanted suburbanites from Middle America some of whom have complicated sexual histories with one another.

As the hostess emerges, naked, from the tent, she walks to the top of a small rise, wraps a large purple towel around herself and says at the top of her voice, "Would you all please be quiet. Some of us are in an altered state of consciousness." How, I wonder, do people in an altered state of consciousness plan to care for the two-year-old and four-year-old?

The hostess is to take a swim in her pool.

My heart and my soul long for God, in a dry and thirsty land where no water is, mused David in the wilderness of Judah. Something in me knows how he felt.

I turn out of the driveway. The lights of Los Alamos sparkle in the dark of the Jemez mountains twelve miles to my right. There—behind the electric glitter, there in the purple black where Robert Oppenheimer went as a boy to summer camp and returned as a man to develop and build the atomic bomb—stand pine trees, homes, schools, churches, nuclear reactors.

I drive up the valley, over the mountain, past the 7,000 feet elevation marker, and head down the road off the Old Taos highway. Noting the landmarks, I wonder if perhaps the guests at the dinner party are in permanent denial about life in the shadow of the bomb. Almost home, I stop at the small bridge at the corner of Cerro Gordo and Upper Canyon. Shutting off the car's engine, and holding onto a tree trunk, I steady myself down to the river to sit for a moment and gather my thoughts.

Melting snow hits the stones, and the light of the rising moon over the ridge makes shadows on the grass beneath my feet. The damp, the closeness, the wind surround me. The quiet cleans my senses. Branches of the willows on the banks help me pull myself back up to the dirt road and the car.

The 23rd Psalm echoes in my mind as I drive up the hill and round the bend.

He makes me lie down in green pastures.

In the green pasture to my left I lay, on mild days, in the grass.

He leads me to water in places of repose; he renews my life.

The river in whose waters our family plays, by whose banks we picnic, bubbles as it runs toward the city.

Though I walk through a valley of deepest darkness . . .

The verse makes me think of the Thai and Cambodian border valleys where I worked as a photojournalist, and of depressions not just geographical but emotional. The snow, the stones, the river, the green pastures, all are specific, illustrative examples to me that dwelling in biblical words is not sentimental longing, but the day-to-day experience of my life.

Only goodness and steadfast love shall pursue me all the days of my life, and I shall dwell in the house of the Lord for many long years.

Meditating on what it might mean to dwell in the house, the consciousness of God, I turn into the driveway and shut off the ignition. A glance at the odometer tells me I live forty-two and a half miles from the intersection of Trinity and Oppenheimer Drive. Checking the mailbox, I walk down the drive to the house fully aware that I live at the intersection of the mystical and the individual and one man's finger away from total annihilation.

My grandson Russell's bike is on the walk, and I remind myself to tell him tomorrow that bikes get parked, not dropped.

Still thinking of the woman channeling the Magdalene, I open the door, take off my shoes and step onto the words of God to Moses painted in black on the white floor:

> *Put off thy shoes from off thy feet,*
> *for the place whereon thou standest*
> *is holy ground.*

PART ONE

One is not born, but becomes, a woman.

SIMONE de BEAUVOIR

CHAPTER 1

Chicago

TRAIN UP A CHILD

A LONG TIME ago, I heard someone say that men fall in love with what they see, women with what they hear. I fell in love with the Bible when it spoke to me. Its words were in my ear in the morning when I rose, in my bed at night.

Words evoke images that appear to me the way a movie occasionally does. I have found myself with Ruth and Naomi on the way between Moab and Bethlehem or empathizing with Mary Magdalene at the reception her report of the Resurrection received.

Through bitterness, through joy, for better or for worse, the Bible is my pastor. It sustains, feeds, leads, lifts, elucidates, mothers and husbands me.

I could say many things about my travels with the Bible. That God is available when turned to for direction.

That spiritual guidance comes directly, without an intermediary.

That the Bible is not a story merely about distant for-eigners and their domination of women but also a report of life in the landscape of the present moment.

That in that report the women in the Bible are most often visited by God in their darkest, least powerful hours.

As a journalist traveling with the Bible, I have inter-viewed thousands of women and men. I have stood with them on the brink of their epiphanies. I have interviewed ministers from Mother Teresa to the television evangelist from Southern California, a former Mrs. America, who preached money as evidence of God before it all became too much for her and she took off for tropical shores. And I have interviewed women from all walks of life quietly working it out as best they could, wondering if they were alone in their search.

I marvel at the ways we try to sort out our relationship with God and with our mothers and fathers—with all the people we meet in life. How does it begin? When does it end, this longing, this transforming struggle to under-stand? Perhaps no one knows. But I believe the answers lie in the joints and marrow of our lives, and, for some, in the difference between the God of the Bible and the God of doctrine and dogma.

In the damp, cavernous basement of St. Philip Nehri Roman Catholic Church, the Adrian Dominican nuns ran a nursery school for children of their South Side Chicago parish. It was there, at three years of age, that I discovered the power of religion over the body.

One day, waiting in line with the other children for milk and cookies, I took plain or chocolate milk. I don't remember which, although I have asked myself many times. I just recall one of my classmates howling that I left her with a flavor she didn't want.

The nuns said nothing and locked me in the coat closet. I was either guilty or the scapegoat, I didn't know which. Scrunched down in the corner with the wet leggings and boots and jackets and fallen mittens, I sat under the naked light bulb, flushed and hot, scared and confused. I only wanted to get home and tell Gwendolyn Ewing what had happened.

Since the day I was born, it seemed, she had been there to feed me, talk to me, explain how things worked; to distinguish hot water from cold, horseradish from mayonnaise, buttons from zippers, block letters from cursive. My mother, also named Gwendolyn, an absent figure, was not the glue of my childhood.

Gwendolyn Ewing would, I knew, explain why there was not enough chocolate or white milk when loaves and fishes fed thousands. I felt her spirit waiting for me through the hour I spent in the closet huddled under the naked light bulb. She would tell me why these ladies in black habits did not think the way that we, she and I, did.

Shortly after school let out at noon, as I pedaled my tricycle home across the alley, I heard car wheels screeching. I turned my head to the right and saw the horrified face of a young Chinese man behind the wheel of the car, just before it hit me. I fell to the ground a few feet from the alley. The wonderful tricycle, which matched my maroon coat with its velvet collar and leggings, lay twisted.

Above me were the branches of the tree in my own front yard, also twisted, gnarled, bare. I recognized the sign of the cross. I lay there, stuck to the earth, transfixed by the sight of the branches against the gray winter sky. Gwendolyn appeared. "Pick yourself up, girl," she said, as she dusted me off and helped me stand. "You don't look hurt to me." She took my hand and walked me into the back yard.

"Get on this swing, child, and swing as high as you can and we'll see if you broke any bones."

Obedient, steadied, I pushed hard and held the chains of the swing tightly in my palms, the cold air in my face.

In the kitchen, carefully placing a few selected Band-aids here and there on my hands and cheeks, Gwendolyn listened to the story of my morning at school: about the light bulb, the coat closet, the chocolate and white milk.

"Now I'm bad," I said. "I'm punished."

"Jesus does not hate anybody, Jesus loves little children especially. You are not bad. You are a child," she answered. "Those nuns are white people. And white people sometimes act in ways that don't make sense."

I, a willful child, she said, must learn to be more careful and help the nuns out when I can.

Resting on her bosom, tears wiped away, redeemed by a woman's love, I accepted everything she said as gospel.

Gwendolyn had been a school teacher in Alabama and spoke with authority. She had the most beautiful handwriting I have seen to this day and she had won awards for her lettering in the Palmer method, which she hung, framed, in her apartment. She was then in her forties, which at the time seemed very old. Her nieces lived in the South, and she had no children. Her husband, the man she followed north to Chicago, had died. Unable to find a teaching job in the city, she took what work the times allowed her, caring for our family, sitting in the kitchen holding me on her lap, feeding me and explaining Jesus' attitudes. We belonged to each other.

I was her only pupil, so Gwendolyn had me reading and carrying on dialogues about a world of subjects as I sat at the white kitchen table with my lunch. I went with Gwendolyn to worship on Sunday mornings and my first church experiences were with her, climbing Jacob's ladder in light, music, exhortations.

That night, Gwendolyn told my father that he should put me in another school. I left the nuns and the question of free will, guilt and punishment and entered the University of Chicago Lab School where the fact that I read books, asked questions, made choices did not seem peculiar, as it had in the basement of the church.

Gwendolyn loved it when I came home from my new school the next Christmas and announced that she had lied to me. Jesus, I said, was a baby and couldn't possibly know about loving everyone. It became one of her family stories about me. She would tell every new friend of mine that she met, repeat it to my mother and her mother.

"Do you remember when she said, 'Jesus ain't nothing but a baby?' "

CHAPTER 2

Chicago

$\mathcal{E}$ V E

MY PARENTS AND grandparents were non-church-going Protestant Scandinavians who left the Lutheran church. The patriarch of my mother's family was Olaf Hoel, a circuit-riding, black-robed, white-ruffle-collared pastor from Norway who ministered throughout the Dakotas, Iowa and western Minnesota. His nine children had sat at the supper table listening to Scripture in Norwegian and English and, as adults, wanted none of it.

The God of my father's father was medicine. Herman Bundesen, M.D. was for over fifty years chief public health officer for Chicago and Cook County. It was his zeal and common sense that kept syphilis rates in Chicago the lowest in the country during the nation's syphilis epidemic of the twenties and thirties. His reputation as the country's leading expert on prenatal and child care was known coast to coast from his long-running columns in newspapers and magazines, and was borne out by the low rate of infant mortality in Chicago. Weekends spent at his home were full of cousins, games and roughhousing with grandfather at the center of every event.

Both my parents thought my interest in religion beside the point in the twentieth century. They were Americans now and used the Episcopal church only for the ceremonies of marriage and burial. I, on the other hand, assumed religion and the church to be the very essence of a life. Perhaps it was the influence of the nuns, perhaps the influence of Gwendolyn. Or perhaps, Jeremiah saw something common to us all when he said, *Before I formed thee in the belly, I knew thee.*

I already believed at the age of twelve that a relationship with God is a singular experience when I went off by myself to be baptised and confirmed. My parents stayed home.

My parents had divorced when I was five and that last year of their marriage I recall as fights, tears, fear. Gwendolyn divided her time between my mother's house and my father's. That year I saw my first death. A boy fell off a truck in front of our apartment and was crushed beneath its wheels. And I read in the papers, and had nightmares each night, about a girl my age who had been murdered, dismembered, her body parts strewn in the city sewer pipes. The message was clear; it was dangerous to be a girl.

———

There was respite when my baby sister (born shortly before my parents separated) and my mother and I moved to my maternal grandparents. There I read in the paper about the ending of the war. There I sat on my grandfather's lap, raked leaves with him in the front yard in the autumn, basked in the serenity of their home until my grandfather's death.

My grandmother Ferne bought back the house she and her husband had sold a few years before, and I moved to a large upper room where I watched through my window the trees blossom and leaf, the leaves turn and fall. I listened to the radio on those days I stayed home from school and we watched football on the television when my uncles, one of whom had played and coached professionally, came to visit from their nearby homes.

We moved again when my mother remarried. It was a new home, in a new suburb. My sister and I shared a room, and when a baby boy arrived he slept in a crib in the room with my mother and stepfather. The nearest church was Methodist and a mile away. I joined the youth group, walking across empty fields that waited silently for the homes that would spring up there. I, too, was empty, waiting for the home my heart longed for to spring up out of some deeper level of earth or heaven.

We sat at small tables, in the recreation room basement of the modern church, singing hymns with missionary zeal, our twelve-to-fifteen-year-old faces red and flushed from a late Sunday afternoon on the ice skating rink. We memorized the names of the books of the Bible—Genesis, Exodus, Leviticus, Numbers, Deuteronomy, Joshua, Judges.

What was inside their pages? Proud as I was that I was learning the names of the books of the Bible, I learned little to shake my presumption that there were two classes of people: men who were ordained, men and all women who were not. Those who followed and those who led. To me, the books of the Bible were historical tomes, readable, at best, in fragments. I wanted more.

A trip with a classmate and his father to see the Harlem Globetrotters play basketball in a local gym was an epiphany. Humans could move, not be constricted, could be poetry. I was a young woman, Scandinavian-American prepubescent, seeing agility, enthusiasm, intricacy that I had not, I thought, seen before. In the spirit of the display on the court, I found community that I had not experienced since church with Gwendolyn.

New worlds opened as they do after epiphanies. I stayed home from school for weeks and watched televised hearings from the nation's capital—gangsters and senators. Good guys and bad. I was enthralled with democracy, with the currency of events. My mother, blessed with a daughter who could baby-sit and who was interested in her one-time college field of studies, political affairs, was glad to humor this interest.

The next American war, the one in Korea, was over. My stepfather was not called up to serve as the naval officer he had been in World War II although we waited every day for the mail in anticipation and apprehension. Secure as a lawyer with a conglomerate, supportive of my near-starvation for education, he moved us to another suburb. Another baby boy was born. We four children moved with my mother and stepfather to the school district where he had been raised on the suburban shores of Lake Michigan.

And I went to high school. Indications of future life are glimpsed in those halls. Two years younger than my classmates, I faded into the landscape of several thousand students until, as the times dictated, I was noticed by a male classmate. But I bored quickly with what the dating scene had to offer and cast my lot with the women who went to church and to temple.

I went almost daily to mass, Episcopal or Roman Catholic, cross of soot marking my forehead on Ash Wednesday, no meat on Fridays. There was no question that God could be visited only through an intermediary, perhaps in wafer and grape juice, in ritual, in an authorized parish world. Or, on the occasions I was invited to temple, through matzoh and bitter herbs.

What was clear to me then was that God was up there somewhere and we, down on earth, were supposed to do certain penitent things to atone for the sin of Eve, the first woman—attend church, remain virgins and be subservient. There we were, adorned with single strands of pearls, worshipping, we were told, an absent and perfect Messiah.

Assigned to give a report on Christian Science and its place in American culture, I visited the local branch of that church. Reading books by and about Mary Baker Eddy for my English report, I discounted the religion. Who, I thought then, Bible unread except in fragments, could possibly believe any woman's report on the nature of Spirit, God?

So under the guidance of male pastors and priests, I memorized liturgy and prayers and went to college desiring God the Father, Maker of all things visible and invisible, not flesh and blood men. Not even the captain of the football team, returned from war in Korea, who took me home to meet his parents and offered me a ring. Not the captain of the basketball team who proposed marriage, not the wrestling coach who came to meet my mother and was somewhat shocked by her heated attention to him.

Family money ran out, I left college and went to work. I was seventeen, had my own apartment, couldn't walk the streets without being propositioned. Although I had never been on a blind date, when my boss suggested meeting her husband's partner I agreed and met the man I was to marry. "He went with my husband to a religious school for six years," the boss said. "He's really a straight arrow."

We agreed to meet in the boss's apartment. She opened the door and two men—one blond, one darker and graying, both wearing suits and ties—were studying architectural drawings spread across the glass coffee table. Neither looked up. Introductions were made. The blond was my boss's husband. And that was the last conversation with the men, who took their dinner plates and settled themselves back in front of the drawings.

"They are both so involved in business I can hardly get their attention," my hostess said as we did the dishes.

"He really liked you," she said the next morning at work. "Let's have dinner again tomorrow."

The distance and silence didn't bother me. It reminded me of my relationship to God.

"I'm going to Arizona with my grandmother to visit my uncle," I said on one of our dinners for four.

"I thought we'd get married," he said. "Maybe one of these days go down to City Hall."

Less than what I wanted, I went with my grandmother.

After a month he called me in Arizona.

"I'm coming out Friday. Get the license, a dress, schedule the wedding."

It seemed the only option on the horizon. His religious

school background tipped the scales. My parents, who were beginning to worry that I would be either a perpetual heart-breaker or a spinster, murmured mild, "how nice's" over the phone. I was two years away from legal age. My father sent written permission.

On the way to the wedding my uncle said, "So what are you using for birth control?"

"Birth control? What's that?"

"Oh, Lord," he said, his eyes on the turn into St. James the Apostle.

The next morning we returned to Chicago.

I was pregnant two months later.

My husband, older by more than a decade, ridiculed my appearance and refused to allow me to go out in public—to church, to school, to dinner. For Christmas, in the sixth month of pregnancy, he gave me a wardrobe of clothes in my prepregnant size eight.

My daughter was born at home—three days after I started labor. I named her Kristin, a Norwegian follower of Christ.

Six weeks afterward, on our first anniversary, I went to dinner to meet, for the first time, men my husband described as business associates. What I knew of his work was an office in the city with gold lettering on the door, Real Estate Investments.

I followed him through the noisy nightclub, past tables

and chairs, party-goers and waiters. A man in a tuxedo stood at a door in the back of the room. He waved his hand in acknowledgment and knocked on the door. It opened. At the far end of a large, darkened, soundproofed room, seated in a straight row at the head of a banquet table, the heirs of Al Capone looked me up and down. I recognized three men—their pictures appeared daily on the front page of the newspapers, faces obscured by their hats or body-guards' hands.

"This is my wife," said my husband.

Motioning in their direction he said to me, "And you know who these men are," as he rattled off their notorious names.

"Oh, and these are their wives."

"I told him," one of the wives was saying, "I"m not gonna let some other woman cash in. I'm gonna live like your second wife. And so I bought this coat," she said, motioning with a laugh toward a dark black, full-length mink draped over a chair beside the dinner table.

Warm milk from nursing breasts leaked through the Kleenex in my bra onto the green faille dress I had bought for the occasion. The white cardigan over my shoulders, studded with pearls, did nothing to keep me warm, nothing to protect me from what could only be described as the cold, hard facts.

*　　*　　*

"There's been an obvious mistake," I said on the drive home. "We'll get a divorce."

"You'll get used to it," he said.

"Daddy, daddy," I said, on the phone the next morning. "You won't believe what happened."

"You married him. You're stuck with him," said my father from the sanctity of his law office.

I called every lawyer I knew.

"Dear," they said to a man, "what does your father say?"

Not one would represent me in a divorce.

I called the police. They said it was a domestic problem. My family didn't believe me or didn't want to know.

Nineteen years old, adolescent expectations crushed, rejected, unheard, I hung up the phone and went down the basement stairs with a handful of laundry. Sitting on the bottom stair, sheets in my arms, I was wretched with certainty that I was at the absolute bottom of my life.

I had been good, I told myself. I was faithful, religious, right-acting and my concept of what was the just reward for the righteous was way out of reach. I was powerless, alone, my own naivete my enemy. I was not the first woman to find herself in enemy territory, but I was there all the same. How had I gotten myself in this fix?

Like Eve in the garden after eating the apple, all I could do was admit my mistake.

But I did not think that because of that mistake I should spend my life at dinner with men warring both with each other and the federal government.

The doorbell rang.

Baby slung on hip, I stood at the opened door and stared. Three women—two of whom had been at the nightclub— announced they wanted to get to know me better.

They followed me into the kitchen, and sat on the small, wire, ice-cream chairs my grandmother had found for me in roadside shops. I put on the coffee pot.

The oldest woman began to explain "our" schedule.

"Saturday nights, see, we all go out with the husbands. Sundays are for the family or whatever. Wednesday is the girls' night out and we usually go bowling or see a show or something like that, and Friday is a good day to get your hair done. Friday night is the men's night out."

I never dreamed of getting my hair done. What if I didn't want to go out on Wednesday nights? Or Saturday, for that matter?

The new face in the group was exotic. Extraordinarily beautiful, with elegant, long, red-painted fingernails, she said she had five children under six, and I didn't see how it was possible to keep such fingernails in an era when all diapers were cloth held together with safety pins. How could she change three babies ten times a day? I was nothing if not practical.

The only grounding I could find was my kitchen shelves. I fixed my eyes on the symbols of my identity as an American homemaker—brown and yellow pixie Peter Pan peanut butter labels, red and white Campbell's soup cans, William Penn staring back at me again and again and again, smaller and smaller and smaller, from the cardboard Quaker Oats box.

Before I could fit into the schedule, I took my daughter and ran away to the haven of my grandmother's house in Minnesota.

Downstairs in the white clapboard, two-story house, my great-aunt Nell and her husband, Ernest, went about their quiet business. Upstairs Ferne Hoel, my mother's mother, was baking or hooking a rug or watching televised baseball while Kristin napped. I was out on the golf course, alone on my grandmother's privately owned nine-hole preserve.

Her home was to the left of the fourth hole as one came up the drive. The white of the house gleamed against the angles and planes of the rolling meadows and fields, kept in pristine condition for my grandmother's May-to-September daily round.

My head was down, shoulders relaxed. The shaft of the club felt as if it were attached to my palm by a smooth and flexible strand. The sound of the club head against the ball was solid, and I followed through the way my grandmother had showed me for the past ten years. I looked up to see the white ball bounce smoothly and surely to within eight feet of the flag. I would be able to make the putt in two strokes.

My back to the house, I fussed with the putter and felt my right arm pull too sharply back. The ball went past the hole and stopped three feet on the other side. I wasn't sure why it mattered that I got this right, why I felt so tense, but I positioned myself carefully, the house by then in front of me slightly to my left. I took a deep breath and slowly pushed the ball. It dropped in and that metal sound rang in my ears. I picked the ball out of the hole and looked up in time to see a large, black car kicking dust up the long drive to the house. In less than a week my husband had found me.

I refused to sleep with him. He beat me. He also arranged for me to model, driving me to assignments, waiting for me, watching me. I refused to take money from him and used the earned income to support my house, myself, my daughter.

He traveled. I fantasized that he might die in a plane crash. I had a one-week affair, got pregnant and although my husband was enraged, though he took a mistress, still he refused to let me go. Or to give up the nightmare life we led where one night there would be laughing and smiling among his friends at dinner and the next morning one of those supposedly happy men would be found in the trunk of a car with various body parts removed. I got sick and took to the safety of a hospital bed.

Eventually it hit me that if I participated in this life at all, even in the least way, I would never get out.

When there is no one else around, it is easier to hear what the next step should be. Don't do any of this, I thought. Don't fight it. Just don't do it.

I named my son Thomas, for the disciple to whom Jesus appeared through a closed door and, who put his hand in the wounds of the resurrected Jesus. By the time I came home with my son from another week's stay of hospital safety I was convinced I would find a way out.

A year later six men sat at my dining room table. Three were from a small town, over a thousand miles away in the Southwest, where, with union pension fund money, a factory was to be built employing hundreds of people. My husband was involved. One grateful small-town man was saying, "We want to give you all houses in our town. We've started to build one."

"I'll take it," I said, passing the roast beef as I looked at the scene in the mirrored wall behind the table.

There was silence in the room.

When everyone left, my husband, red-faced, yelled, "Why did you do that? You know I am buying us a house," and he named a far, expensive suburb.

My response was, "No. You can kill me, or have me killed, but I will not live like this, like the wives of your friends. I will not occupy a mausoleum in the suburbs and dress for Saturday night display."

I meant it and it strikes me as strange now, to think of the simple sincerity with which I was ready to lay down my life.

All else had failed. I had nowhere else to go, except the wilderness.

CHAPTER 3

Deming

I SAIAH

IN MY EARLY twenties I lived with my children in a house on the edge of a cotton field thirty miles from Mexico. My husband visited once every six weeks. The mountains were miles away on three sides, but to the south the land was so flat that eyes sharp enough, trained enough, that knew what they were looking for, could see to the border. There was a roadhouse and bar between the political boundaries of the two countries, and then, for another hundred or so miles, little but earth and poverty.

Even when husbands are cruel or liars, or any number of other wearing combinations, many women, through the ages, have still listened to their men.

I had given up on church. I had discovered a compelling reason not to be married and not to obey my husband. Yet my husband, oozing hypocrisy, said, "If it's all so terrible for you why don't you read the Bible?"

*   *   *

Cornered, my only recourse was to the field of the self. And so, one night, sitting at my desk, scanning the Bible, looking for understanding, exhausted by worry over my son's asthma, I tried to sort out the puzzle of how, why this Book held meaning. Then I heard it.

Enlarge the place of thy tent, and let them stretch forth the curtains of thine habitations: spare not, lengthen thy cords, and strengthen thy stakes; For thou shalt break forth on the right hand and on the left.

Who was this Isaiah speaking to me?

What was this still small voice speaking with such authority that the whole scene in front of me changed? I had sat down in familiar surroundings to look seriously into a basically unfamiliar, dauntingly opaque text. Like countless millions of men and women who have found themselves unexpectedly in extreme and unnatural circumstances, I needed power beyond the most powerful.

Moved outside myself by the voice, the glass door slipped away—as did the living room, my children sleeping, my sense of who I was and what I was doing—replaced by nothing but the Book in front of me and singular stars hung in the space of a full night. I could count them one by one, register their brightness, monitor them as they flickered, gaze at them spread across the sky. There was no mediator between me, the Book and my perception.

For the mountains shall depart, and the hills be removed; but my kindness shall not depart from thee.

Fear not; for thou shalt not be ashamed: neither be thou confounded; for thou shalt not be put to shame.

The words that I heard from the Bible said forget that I am a woman that a man knows, blames, causes to suffer. Forget that I have no way out and no place to go outside the house on the edge of the cotton field. Forget my self and time.

I had been educated to think that only saints and prophets heard disembodied speech. Who was I to think the Bible is a talking book?

I didn't know then that God regularly visits powerless women.

It seemed natural to follow the voice. I merely looked in the back of the Bible to the Concordance and with those words, "tent" and "enlarge," began a long journey with the men and women whose stories are told in the Bible.

And the Lord appeared unto him in the plains of Mamre: and he sat in the tent door in the heat of the day; And he lifted up his

*eyes and looked, and, lo, three men stood by him: and when he saw
them, he ran to meet them from the tent door, and bowed himself
toward the ground.*

I was certainly not Abram, described in Genesis as sitting in the tent door in the heat of the day. I had no
thought that it was the Lord that spoke to me, no presumption of anything at all I had known as religious. The
moment held no informed speculation. It was not the heat
of the day but the medium warm of a desert night. And
there were no men, no people at all. Nothing but stars and
quiet space, replacing my paralysis, promising me something if I took action.

What stands out is how effortless, how normal it seemed.
My body, instead of being jerked to and fro by forces I
didn't understand, seemed fetterless. But the only similar-
ity that I could draw between the story of Abram and my
own experience was that I had heard a voice, left off sitting
in my house and was now, somehow in thought, outside,
looking around.

I slept that night. No checking on my son, no up and
down, just sleep. The morning brought the sight of Tom,
full, pink, plump. Gone was the fragile, dull-skinned child
that I had tucked in his crib.

I have thought often of that evening—not so much of
what happened but of what didn't happen. There was no

particular excitement, no music, no rustle of wings, no great flash of light. But in that next morning the light did seem clearer than the day before, and Tom was well. I couldn't wait to get back to the Book.

Isaiah had a lot to say I discovered, while the children were napping or sometimes when they were playing in their small pool in the patio on the hot nights of summer in the desert.

Ho, everyone that thirsteth, come ye to the waters, and he that hath no money; come ye, buy, and eat; yea, come, buy wine and milk without money and without price.

For my thoughts are not your thoughts, neither are your ways my ways . . .

For ye shall go out with joy, and be led forth with peace: the mountains and the hills shall break forth before you into singing, and all the trees of the field shall clap their hands.

As one whom his mother comforteth, so will I comfort you; and ye shall be comforted in Jerusalem.

Picturing myself an immigrant, Bible in hand, searching for some promised land, was not a stretch. Who does not think that good is far off, in some other place or time? Thirsting for justice, my own thinking seriously inadequate to my occasion, I pored over the King James Version of the Bible.

In its world were women; solitary, not heard, upset, in strange, dangerous and confined circumstances, like myself. Biblical women hid their children from dangerous men and political policies. Captive slave girls talked back to kings. A woman led an army in war. In the Bible women acted, not just in subservience or disobedience to men but independently of men.

Biblical promises were for everyone who thirsted, mountains broke forth with singing and trees clapped their hands—all without regard to gender. God comforted as a mother and to top it off I read that God's rain fell impartially—on the just and unjust.

Yes, I said to myself. Yes. This is what I want to hear.

Enlarging the borders of my tent began in small ways. I moved my desk into the bedroom, the bed into the living room. For the first time with a room of my own, my mother dead nearly a year, my father a thousand miles away, and no one there to interpret to my imperfect understanding, looking up words and reading what struck me, following where I was led became my way of seeing.

The human mind revises, casts favorable or unfavorable

light on its past, present and future. What I learned then and what I know now, what I knew then but had forgotten, often blurs. But I look back and see myself in the room with the rust brown shag carpet, put there with some notion of the practicality of the color. I can feel the width of the desk, the pencil and pad of paper to my left, the Bible and a new Cruden's Concordance in front of me, a clock, wooden and antique, with a farm scene painted on its glass face and given to me by my grandfather Bundesen, to the right. It was a time of self-definition.

I began at the beginning.

There were different stories of Creation in just the first three chapters of the Bible. The first described an active process of six days and a seventh of rest. This Creation was full of activity initiated by the Spirit. There was movement, speech, sight, light, dividing, gathering, bringing forth. There was grass, seed, fruit. There were signs, seasons, moving creatures, male and female created simultaneously, blessings, dominion, and, it seemed to me, a Creator who looked at it all, saw that it was good, gave a deep sigh and rested.

But there—in the sixth verse of the second chapter of Genesis—was an entirely other story, as in a parallel universe. A mist rises up from the earth and within that mist another God, another story of Creation, not at all the same as the first. In the beginning spiritual creation and on the heels of that a material creation—the one I was sure I lived in every day.

With no knowledge of when these stories were written, or who wrote them, no pastor or priest to interpret for me, I assumed that they were there in meaningful order. I supposed that if I didn't live in the first Creation I must live in the second where man is made out of dust.

And the Lord God formed man of the dust of the ground, and breathed into his nostrils the breath of life; and man became a living soul.

This creation is not only second—it is a reversal of the first order, where male and female are made after Light and waters are divided from waters, dry land from seas, after plants, fowls of the air and great whales.

This poor dust creature stands, in emptiness, and then this Lord God makes a garden eastward in Eden, four rivers, some animals and temptation.

And the Lord God commanded the man, saying, Of every tree of the garden thou mayest freely eat: But of the tree of the knowledge of good and evil, thou shalt not eat of it; for in the day that thou eatest thereof thou shall surely die.

Creation One, as I came to call it in my desktop notes, doesn't mention evil or death—one reason it is so handily discounted as the myth. In Creation Two, out of the ground, not out of Spirit, come plants and animals and, during a Lord God–induced deep sleep, an unnamed woman from the rib of a man. On the face of it both stories, for different reasons, are hard to believe and may be the reason that theology argues so strongly for a faith that is often suspension of disbelief.

The woman, later named Eve by her husband, made from a dust-man who was sleeping, the product of a dream, acts, not out of knowledge of herself as the full expression of the Glory of God, not as coevolving partner in Creation. I could safely say I did not feel as if I were a coevolving partner in Creation. The picture I had of myself was as of Eve.

There was no particular biblical genesis to the snake. But there it was, suggesting that a taste of the knowledge of both good and evil would turn the woman in the garden into something like one of the gods—who so far haven't been mentioned.

For God doth know that in the day ye eat thereof, then your eyes shall be opened and ye shall be as gods, knowing good and evil. And when the woman saw that the tree was good for food, and that it was pleasant to the eyes, and a tree to be desired to make one wise, she took of the fruit thereof, and did eat, and gave also to her husband with her; and he did eat.

And the eyes of them both were opened, and they knew that they were naked.

Like Eve, the woman born out of a deep sleep, I had thought something—to her a good-looking fruit to make her wise and to me marriage—looked safe enough. Like Eve, I was wrong. Like Eve, I knew it.

There was to be no help in the history I had read. I had been taught that women out of the fold had been burned at the stake. Nor was there solace in the literature I had read in school. "God is thy law, thou mine; to know no more/Is woman's happiest knowledge," Milton's *Paradise Lost* proclaims.

Cutting to the chase, in despair, I looked at the last two chapters of the Bible to find out the ending. Revelation was my only hope.

And I saw a new heaven and a new earth: for the first heaven and the first earth were passed away; and there was no more sea. And I John saw the holy city, new Jerusalem, coming down from God out of heaven, prepared as a bride adorned for her husband.

And I heard a great voice out of heaven saying, Behold the tabernacle of God is with men, and he will dwell with them, and they shall be his people, and God himself shall be with them, and be their God. And God shall wipe away all tears from their eyes; and there shall be no more death, neither sorrow, nor crying, neither shall there be any more pain; for the former things are passed away. And he that sat upon the throne said, Behold, I make all things new.

This was a message to warm the heart of any woman in any era, and it occurred to me that a new heaven and new earth were resolutions of the paradox encountered in the first chapters. At the very least there was to be no more sea from the first chapter and no more death from the second.

A verse in the last chapter echoed with enough precision to give me yet more rest. It was the same theme I had heard earlier from Isaiah.

Ho, everyone that thirsteth, come ye to the waters, and he that hath no money: come ye, buy, and eat: yea, come, buy wine and milk without money and without price.

John's recording in Revelation says,

And the Spirit and the bride say, Come. And let him that heareth say, Come. And let him that is athirst come. And who-soever will, Let him take of the water of life freely.

In the beginning spiritual creation and on the heels of that a material creation—a different creation. From my view on the edge of the cotton field, these two versions sat side by side from Eve on—through the lives and times of biblical women.

The two versions end in a Holy City adorned as a bride. It's a place I want to live.

*O*UT OF EGYPT

THERE WAS, THERE in my desert yard, a concrete wall
eight feet high, which met the corners of the house and
extended twelve feet beyond it. Gray block, unpainted,
standing solely to break the force of the desert wind and
sand from cutting into the house, the wall reminded me
that I was a woman shut up in prison.

Standing alone in the yard with the laundry basket, I
picked up a wet sheet and pinned one white corner to the
clothesline. Before I could spread the fabric the distance to
the next clothes pin, the sheet was dry. I knew there was
heat in the desert and waste places of the howling wilderness but I also knew that this was impossible. There are,
after all, laws of physics.

But not then, not there. I looked at the sheet again and
I saw instead women, wrapped in white, kneeling by a
river, washing linens. They were at some distance and

seemed to be suspended by the flowing river that appeared
somewhere beyond my wall where no river existed before.
They were talking and washing and smiling at the water,
but I heard no sound; they saw me, but gave no particular
notice, as if they had always been there both seeing and not
seeing me.

What I was looking for relentlessly was a way out of a self
that is gender, sociological, an object, out of my politically
and emotionally naive self, out of the marriage. Instead
what I saw was a distant view of some women like myself.
I reiterated the actions of other unnamed women washing
sheets in a world waiting to be seen through the stones and
blocks of the wall. I stood on the edge between order and
chaos. And I felt the spillover effect of Resurrection.

For seven long years, I had stood at the tomb of my own
life, and as I picked up the laundry basket with sheets
unhung yet dry, I turned and walked back into the house,
knowing mystery and that, in some significant and sightful
way, I was moved to a different time and a different place.

It is the direct relationship between this event and the
next that from that day on caused me to put store in a world
far simpler than mere physics. I had glimpsed a world of
fractal dimension where the power of unnamed women
could disentangle the past and offer a future—revealed moment by indivisible present moment.

That very night my husband, a hundred pounds heavier

and six inches taller than me, infuriated by my calm, broke down a door to beat me and my son. As I stood there, tearless and silent, he struck me again, and then he stopped, looked at me and left.

The children and I sat at the kitchen counter at three in the morning and ate corn flakes floating in milk and sprinkled with sugar. We ate corn flakes in remembrance of new birth. It was the first food I had taken after Tom's birth.

My husband returned at dawn with two men, called me names, and, after seven years of threatening my life, said that I could leave. He took the children. I waited for weeks in frantic desperation before he returned.

"I'm here to get their clothes and toys," he said. "Why don't you come outside and take a look at my new car."

This form of insanity was not for me.

"There is no milk," I said. "You pack, I'll have the children show me the car and then I'll go to the store and get milk. The children can eat while you get their things."

It's hard to believe that he would leave the children alone with me while he packed but the ego of one who believes he has power blinds the eye.

Parking my car in front of the store, a child in each hand, I turned and looked toward the mountains. It was as if I could see through them to the other side. The wind whispered in the silver and gold light.

For the mountains shall depart, and the hills be removed; but my kindness shall not depart from thee. Fear not; for thou shalt not be ashamed; neither shall thou be confounded; for thou shalt not be put to shame:

For ye shall go out with joy, and be led forth with peace: the mountains and the hills shall break forth before you into singing, and all the trees of the fields shall clap their hands.

I never went back with the milk. I left the desert with two children, twenty dollars, and my passport to freedom, the Bible I kept in the glove compartment.

I thought that being out of my husband's sight and crossing a state boundary meant I was free. How little we know of spiritual progression or of the struggle to stop looking for God and to let God find us. Or of the cost.

Standing in a small Southern California park, pushing first Kristin, then Tom, on swings there, a woman, me, understood what it meant to be alone. Alone was not empty. It was unconditional.

Each woman finds her own way. How I found shelter is not the way another might find food and lodging. How I found employment would not be the way another woman's needs were met. But in the years spent enlarging my tent I had gone back to school. And to church. I remembered as

I took the children off the swings, dusted off their hands and knees and headed back to the car, that in church I had met a couple who lived not far from where I stood.

The thought that I would need a place to stay, that I must find work, had not crossed my mind in the exhilaration of leaving the wilderness. Any land would be a Promised Land. The couple took us in.

The newspaper carried an ad for a teacher in a small religious school. I taught art studies for a time in the school near the Pacific Ocean. My children were enrolled there. Needing more income, I modeled fashions during the department store lunch hour, took another part-time job with a newspaper. After taking the students to art exhibits, I would write about the show.

Scouting an exhibit one day, I fell in love.

The object of my immediate attention was an exquisitely designed land yacht—a sailboat for the sand and desert. I loved the idea and the implementation, and I thought readers of the paper would too. The designer was charming, handsome, well-traveled, wise, single, devoted. During the year we saw each other, with his encouragement, I left my teaching job and took one with the Urban League, writing speeches and then editing a magazine on minority politics.

Donald gave me new perspective on life with a man, but like Lot's wife, I looked back at where I had been and not toward where I was going. My father—in phone calls and a visit—reminded me of my past history. Church friends advised me against marrying someone outside the immediate group. Influenced, choosing timid conservatism, I rejected the proposal of marriage.

By the time I had come to my senses, Donald was looking toward marriage to someone else. I was left with a horrible feeling I'd abandoned the winds of Spirit. Unable or unwilling to forgive myself, this behavior of uncertainty became a pattern in my life. Knowing my ex-husband could find and follow me and my children anywhere, I chose not to inflict that burden on a new husband.

Donald had given me a camera and showed me how to use it. "You have a great eye," he would say. "You will miss the visual world spending all your time in front of a typewriter. Use the camera, record what you see."

So for the next two decades I did, traveling around the United States for magazines and newspapers, always with my children by my side.

CHAPTER 5

Chicago

BUILDING A TABERNACLE

MANY QUESTION TO this day just why the Israelites followed Moses out of Egypt. Some say it was because he had beaten Pharaoh and the magicians at their own game of magic. Others still credit God, the I Am, that led them, troubled and complaining, into the wilderness and through the Red Sea.

There is no question, however, that the women Exodus records as having gone through the parted sea to the promised land with Miriam and her brothers, Aaron and Moses, helped build the tabernacle. They worked, not because they were slaves, but because they wanted to.

And they came, every one whose heart stirred him up, and every one whom his spirit made willing. . . . And they came, both men and women, as many as were willing hearted.

Among other things, some of them gave their mirrors to be hammered down into *the laver of brass, and the foot of it brass, of the lookingglasses of the women assembling, which assembled at the door of the tabernacle of the congregation.*

The tabernacle described in Exodus was an elaborate tent housing the ark of the covenant. Building it was prayer made visible. The women on that journey changed their mirrors into a receptacle for water. In that water, vision— not of physical appearance but spiritual persona—would be reflected.

The women on that journey, Exodus records, who were willing to work side by side with the men, helped to build the shelter for the organizing principles of their society: the Ten Commandments. It is hard to think that this is a career they planned, hard to imagine a resume that says:

Work Experience: Exchanging the physical concept of myself for a more spiritual one. Giving thanks for God's forgiveness and mercy through work.

Specific duties: Hammering down mirrors in to lavers, building a tabernacle.

Except in that most rare world of a small group of people with One God, a woman needs a resume.

In my twenties my work experience read:

Baby-sitter, after-school job at the local newspaper during my second year of high school, nursery school aide, six months as a researcher in a law firm, six months in a weight-loss salon as an "assistant manager" (a title designed to create the illusion of career as the vibrating tables were designed to create the illusion that overeating could be shaken off passively while reclining on a shaking table) and a year and a half of wearing expensive clothes on runways, in front of still and television cameras.

Now, in my early thirties, my resume was a portfolio of pictures of human life reflected in the activities of men, women, children, rich and poor, known and unknown of all colors and beliefs. There was no end to this work.

The Book of Revelation says,

And I heard a great voice out of heaven saying, Behold the tabernacle of God is with men, and he will dwell with them, and they shall be his people, and God himself shall be with them, and be their God.

John's report offers echoes of an earlier report in Exodus.

Then a cloud covered the tent of the congregation, and the glory of the Lord filled the tabernacle. And when the cloud was taken up from over the tabernacle, the children of Israel went onward in all their journeys: But if the cloud were not taken up, then they journeyed not till the day that it was taken up.

Still very much in a cloud of emotion, looking for approval from my father, I was back in Chicago on assignment. Gwendolyn stood by the door, listening as my father—tall, elegant as always in his English tweed suit—gave me the latest news about his country club across the South Shore drive. Gwendolyn said nothing as he described vying buyers of the property: Elijah Mohammed, the Black Muslim leader, and the Chicago Park District.

After seventy-five years as a private sanctuary for white doctors, lawyers, businessmen and their wives and children, the club had reached a crossroad. The members, most of whom had moved to the North Side or the suburbs, were afraid to drive into what had become the black South Side.

The acres and acres of golf greens, the sand and the beach fronting the lake had become worth more in money than in privacy and leisure. The club stood like a great, gray ghost, memories of weddings and coming-out parties and Christmas dinners fading with the death of each club member. The elegance of the club my paternal grandfather helped found, where his six children played tennis, lingered. But the riding trails were seldom used and where hundreds of young women and men in their jodhpurs and hats rode in the autumn horse shows only a few dozen riders appeared.

I came to this conversation as a reporter writing a magazine story about what the club's sale would mean to the city. My father, naturally thinking of me not as a reporter but as his daughter, was pleased that one of his family would write the article to reflect his point of view.

Gwendolyn watched and listened amidst the antiques and the gilded oil portraits in the spacious room, as my father explained that there really was no racial problem here. The now black neighborhood wouldn't mind if the Park District and not a black group owned the property. The Irish-Catholic members of the club who had cousins on the Park District Board would be delighted.

"Go talk to Jim," my father said. "He runs the gas station next door where we park the car. He'll tell you that all this talk about black power and activism is just a few trouble makers. He's our friend."

"Those (expletive)," Jim said, "treat us like we weren't here, like we weren't alive. Pay us to come in there to the club to tow their Lincolns and Chryslers and never let us beyond the driveway."

Staring at the green and the private beach, denied him all his fifty years, Jim warmed to his subject.

"Your daddy don't know," he said. "Honey, white folks

live in their own world. I'd love to see their faces when Elijah Mohammed owns this station and that place across the street."

I walked down to the newsstand on the corner where we used to buy ice cream and where now, my father's son, my brother Brian, stopped on his way home from St. Philip Nehri. Posters, photographs of Elijah Mohammed, were plastered all over the walls. Not surprisingly, the man behind the counter thought it would be a blatant act of racism if a white development group or the white Parks Board bought the property.

When my father learned what I had heard from Jim, and that the newspaper intended to print it, he rushed home from his office as if I were twelve and had been caught shoplifting at Woolworth's. He took me in the den and seated me on the red velvet sofa in front of the hunt pictures bought on a trip to London. He stood before me as if he were arguing a case in court, cross-examining a witness for the opposition.

"I represent the club," he said. "I am a member and you cannot print what these people you have talked to say."

I told him I had to. I am a reporter. I have a job and it's my assignment to report varying perspectives. I am trying to paint a picture of changing times. I was also trying to make a living and pay my children's school tuition.

His pride dissolved into frustration. He was the one who

suggested I do the interview with Jim. Moreover, he had encouraged my path in journalism, adding his own set of Nikons to the camera Donald had given me. He never anticipated this betrayal.

Gwendolyn was ironing, my father's shirt draped over the board, steam floating up with a small hiss as the iron went down and up again. I am seated at the desk, behind the typewriter, so that we can be together while we work.

"You should know better," she said. "This is who your parents are. This is what I have seen and this is what you should know. You are walking in dangerous places."

Until the sun went down and the room darkened, she told me my family history. Gwendolyn reported her educated perspective from the place of an almost but not quite member of the family. Compassion was her keynote.

My mother she described as a beauty, spirited but dampened by her looks, brains, culture and motherhood. My father, caught perhaps in the shadow of his powerful father, a man living in a time when all family expectations were focused on men, all problems theirs to solve, all decisions their burden to make.

"They do not see me, except for how I serve them," she says.

I know this to be true.

"They have forgiven you more than you know," she said. "And I have forgiven you more than you know. No one ever really knows everything that goes on inside someone else. You are responsible only for and to yourself. You must not lie or sway the facts to please. You must stop being disobedient. It is time for you to obey the First Commandment. God requires you to have no other gods. It is time for you to stand by yourself."

I listened quietly, asking no questions. Gwendolyn stood, half in and half out of the shadow. Talking about the years she spent watching out for me, for my mother and father and grandmother, praying and constantly forgiving sins of omission and commission, she wrapped me in the truth. It was her last gift. When she died the next month I was left to begin standing on my own after thirty-three years of her love.

Millions of children in each generation are cared for and influenced more by the language and beliefs of the women who care for them on a daily basis than by their mothers. So it was with me. My political perspectives were Gwendolyn's, not my parents'. My idea of what constituted a Christian unfolded out of her life. My alliance was with her God, and her God, I knew, had led people out of Egypt.

CHAPTER 6

Washington, D.C.

A WOMAN OF THE CITY

LUKE, IN THE seventh chapter of his gospel, describes an unnamed woman, *a woman in the city, who was a sinner,* who washes Jesus' feet with her tears.

Imagine the scene.

Jesus is having dinner with some high priests in a room with high ceilings and whitewashed walls. An unnamed woman enters, carrying an alabaster box of ointment. She walks over to Jesus, stands at his feet and weeps.

Luke does not say how long she wept but he does say that she dried Jesus' feet with her hair and that she kissed and perfumed them.

Jesus used the woman's actions as an example.

Her sins, which are many, are forgiven; for she loved much.

In a pattern of the woman's actions, Jesus washes his disciples' feet at the Passover meal Christians call the Last Supper.

Life in my thirties was full, with a variety of assignments and trips, healthy children, poems and flowers and suitors who gave me all that I missed in a young, unhappy marriage. I enrolled in a master's degree program, owned a house of my own, moved to the nation's capital. The borders of my tent continued to enlarge. Still, bending down in a speechless state of tears would not have been an inappropriate response to the mixture of life then.

I felt like *a woman in the city who was a sinner.* In no particular order, I was confused and conflicted by contemporary sexual mores, my father was ill and dying, Kris and Tom were in their mid-teens. My ex-husband had a Mercedes-Benz delivered to my door. Men followed me down the street and I wasn't sure why or who they were. I thought I knew who I was, and what I knew was that I was in emotional and physical danger. Fearful, confused, humiliated by my own temperamental behavior, I broke my engagement to a man I had met, taken in my house and loved.

There was another even more essential element of conflict. I had stopped listening directly to the words of the

Bible. I became a dependent, listening instead to an over-worked minister's interpretation. I had crossed the fine line between illumination and domination and lost, I thought, the ability and right to hear the Word for myself. I wept for the distances between glimpses of spiritual reality.

Unaware of the suspicion and jealousy that sometimes dog a woman working out her life in what appear to the untrained eye to be enviable circumstances, it was hard to separate what was being thought of me from what I thought of myself; hard to tell tares from wheat and harder still to think of when or what the harvest of my life might be.

I photographed the comings and goings of Presidents, the Congress, the Secretary of State, sports heroes, men and women who are the news. A press photographer in the nation's capital takes a visual record of the court and the courtiers. A photographer is the representative of the person not there.

There is much clamor but little joy in the circumscribed ritual of press conferences. There is scant vibrancy and a certain dullness in the endless rounds of the journalist's response to managed news. Press conferences and assignments are scheduled at the same time as children's school programs. Photographs, which are most people's prized possessions, among the few things they take with them when forced, for some reason, to leave their homes in a few hours, have less and less meaning the more they are staged or controlled.

Paradoxically free but not free, I'd spent several months basically sitting on the living room sofa, my head covered in a scarf, listening to Puccini. Mimi's death scene became the only sound I heard. On the emotional edge, I looked into the light streaming through the high windows of that Georgetown house and longed for that unnamed woman's singleness of purpose.

Photography is language without the tongue. I put away my Nikons and my Canons and the Leica I'd acquired for personal photographic note-taking. I put off the equipment used by my male colleagues on our daily "photo opportunities" in the White House, and gave up my father's hope that I might be a female Karsh of Ottawa, married and settled, perhaps in Idaho.

Reading the daily newspaper was trance inducing. It reveled in the respecting of persons. Day after day the same faces appeared in its pages. The President, proximity to the President, power brokers, proximity to power brokers, occupied the paper's first section. The overwhelmingly black population of Washington was recorded in a separate section. Divinity, I was convinced, didn't see it that way.

So, one day, in the bright morning light, I folded up the paper and ceased reacting to the management of images.

I bought, not an alabaster jar of ointment, but a box camera, 2¼ by 2¼. I began to translate equipment into ideas, to discover photography as ministry.

Translating biblical texts as I understood them in relationship to my life took on the dimension of Zen practice.

The ground glass of the camera on which I was to focus had, like the Holy City of the Book of Revelation, four equal sides. That glass, rather than Washington itself, became my city. The focal point of the picture was found in the Golden Triangle of the Greeks or, I hoped, in the center of the triangle of the Father, Son and Holy Spirit. I would have to, with a 2¼ camera fixed on a tripod, look into the city and through the mirror up to the person being photographed with my head bowed.

I used no flash, only available light, and wore, not a white robe, if in fact that is what the unnamed woman wore, but a black, three-piece man's suit. I cut my hair off like a boy's, and wore no jewelry. Longing to be transparent, I settled for a constant, as low-impact an image as possible.

"You will have to excuse her," seventeen-year-old-Kristin would say to people who could not understand what I was doing or why, "Mother is working it out for eternity." Then she would smile and shake her head.

The disciple Peter, reflecting on a vision that had come to him in a trance, said,

Of a truth I perceive that God is no respecter of persons: But in every nation he that feareth him, and worketh righteousness, is accepted with him.

My take on Peter's statement was a simple one. The citizenship I was looking for was to be found in commitment to God.

I had known since childhood that authentic people come in all colors, did all kinds of work. And I had known life in a small American town.

I photographed the garage mechanic who fixed the car of the man I loved, I photographed the President's chief of staff, the policeman on our beat, the nation's leading party giver, the child next door, a child heir to an empire, my butcher and the man who delivered the wood for our fireplace, the coach of the football team, the gossip columnist at the newspaper. I went to where the archetypes and the specific people who gave the city its character lived and worked and recorded them in black and white and all their shades of gray as they wanted to be seen.

Photographing the known and the unknown as both individuals and representatives of the culture became my way of reconciling my inner and outer life.

I had learned that citizenship meant the daily practice of self-government and self-control.

I had also learned that the desires of the heart bubble to the surface.

PART TWO

And to the woman were given two wings of a great eagle, that she might fly into the wilderness, into her place, where she is nourished for a time, and times, and half a time, from the face of the serpent.

And the earth helped the woman, and the earth opened her mouth, and swallowed up the flood which the dragon cast out of his mouth.

REVELATION 12: 14, 16

CHAPTER 7

Southern China

THE ETERNAL MOTHER

INSIGHT COMES IN a rush. But knowing even a small part of yourself takes experience and practice.

Not long after the nation's bicentennial, after the fireworks and picnics and euphoria, after Kristin had gone off to college and Tom to boarding school, a friend's husband called with an extra visa to the People's Republic of China. I didn't hesitate. Picking up the visa at his law office, I walked around the corner to the airline ticket office, handed over the credit card that had arrived the day before in the mail, and bought an around-the-world ticket.

The next day I left the United States and ventured into China with several cameras, a hundred rolls of film, two Brahms symphonies on tape, two pairs of jeans, a black shirt, three skirts, a toothbrush, hairbrush, my naivete and a Bible.

I arrived the day Madame Mao was arrested and spent a month hitchhiking around the southern part of the country photographing the wall posters that signaled the end of the cultural revolution. I made my home in a hotel room with a canopy bed, a dresser, a chair and table, and floor-to-ceiling windows overlooking a courtyard where chickens ate, laundry dried, old women sat and smoked.

One day fell into the next as I wandered in the streets of Kwangchow.

No neon signs told me what to buy, or where to go. No subliminal or overt messages to be anything, feel or think anything intruded. Without guides or propaganda in my language I was on my own, relying on my own instincts and judgments, never before so peaceful and free.

Youths who had never seen a white woman touched my skin, glaring occasionally in fear but never lust. For the first time since the age of twelve I walked into the streets, not afraid a man would pursue or harass me, or have me with his eyes. Alone in a nation that did not view me as a sexual or economic commodity, I learned that the danger I felt in the nation of my birth was not of my making. It went with the territory.

For the mountains shall depart, and the hills be removed; but my kindness shall not depart from thee.

Fear not; for thou shalt not be ashamed; neither shall thou be confounded; for thou shall not be put to shame.

Isaiah's promise to me, seated at my desk years ago, continued to fulfill itself in enlarged tents, boundaries dissolved and rearranged.

One Sunday I packed my bag and got on a bus. For several hours I rode with the other passengers going into the countryside. Finally the driver motioned me to get off.

We were in the middle of a rice field. After the bus pulled away not a single person could be seen. I walked for several kilometers and found a rock to sit on. In the distance more rice fields shimmered; beyond, a cloud draped over a mountain. Faintly I could see an old woman working alone in a field. My camera recorded the scene, although I knew that no photograph could recapture the space, the color, the feeling.

In near darkness, Mother Earth fed me as she had all the women who have worked there before. I wept. How could I have thought that only change and concrete and technology were my heritage? I had never before felt such completeness, alone yet so warm and comforted.

Thy mother is like a vine in thy blood, planted by the waters: she was fruitful and full of branches by reason of many waters.

———

My mother, I thought, would have loved this freedom and been glad that I had these hours and the peace we never shared when she was alive to the flesh of my youth. Mother Love swept across my sight and with it the knowledge that Gwendolyn, my grandmothers, my mother, my daughter, myself, the woman in the field, all of us, were inseparably cared for by this Impartial Beneficence.

On this Sabbath, in this landscape, all the blessings and dangers of my life mingled with the last light.

After nightfall, cleansed by tears and reflection, I followed a path for another kilometer through a small village, across a bridge. An armed guard stood at a fork in the road. Taking the other path, I walked through a forest of trees with taller, smoother trunks than I had ever seen before, perfectly pruned and cut with leaves lacing the darkened sky, through an arch leading into what looked like a small palace.

When I asked about sleeping accommodations, a man at the door assured me that there was a room waiting for me even though I did not know I would be there, and I had not been followed or watched. He led me to the first room up a small flight of steps. It had a canopy bed, a fifteen-foot square bathroom and a tub four feet wide and six feet deep. A balcony hung over the river.

The man came into the room and wordlessly filled the

tub with steaming hot mineral water. He left a pot of tea.
I suspected from the presence of the guard at the fork in the
road that this was a military retreat, a place of mineral baths
and rest, the Chinese version of Camp David, the American
Presidential retreat. I climbed into the tub with my Bible,
tea and simple wonder.

*O Lord, thou hast searched me and known me. Thou knowest
my downsitting and my uprising, thou understandest my thought
afar off. Thou compassest my path and my lying down, and art
acquainted with all my ways. Whither shall I go from thy spirit?
or whither shall I flee from thy presence? If I take the wings of the
morning and dwell in the uttermost parts of the sea; Even there
shall thy hand lead me, and thy right hand shall hold me. For
thou hast possessed my reins; thou hast covered me in my mother's
womb.*

The words of the Psalm floated through my pores as the
hot water washed against my buoyant body.

Traveling with the Bible was not lonely. Solitary, but
not lonely. I emerged from the safety of China into Hong
Kong a week later with thousands of pictures, my belong-
ings, presents for the children and the distinct feeling that
my life was changing.

Two men waited for me at the Hong Kong train station, both Americans, both named Gene. One was the lawyer who provided me with the visa; the other was a journalist who wanted my story and pictures on China for his paper.

Lunch on the veranda of the Repulse Bay Hotel with the journalist. Dinner at a table for two in the revolving restaurant atop the Hong Kong Regent with the lawyer. A day-long trip on a private ship cruising to outlying islands and an afternoon picnic with the lawyer. A plane ride over those same islands with the journalist capped by a midnight ride on the ferry across the harbor.

I may have looked like an independent woman balancing attractive options. But emotionally I was still the teenager whose sophomore theme had been "A Ship in Harbor Is Always Safe" and who had returned toward a strict adherence of the commandment—"Thou shalt not commit adultery."

Where once I had found justification for adultery, now I couldn't think about a present or a future with a married man, a friend's husband, even on the edge of divorce, as the lawyer was.

"I don't live here anymore," I said when the taxi pulled up in front of my Washington house. I shook hands with married Gene, who had been on the same plane with me, and walked in to hear the phone ringing. It was the other Gene, the journalist, from some place in Thailand.

"Come back," he said. "Come back."

Kristin was at college; Tom a junior boarding at high school.

And so, after Christmas holiday with my children and my father and family in Chicago, I did.

Gene met me with champagne, a limousine and the news that he had been assigned to the Philippines—and arranged for me to go with him to Manila.

"Try it for a few weeks," he said. "Please try it."

This sounds like material not from a life but from a novelized version of a life. Champagne, limousines, strange lands, adoring lover, and, if I hadn't experienced it, I might envy it. And this novelized version might have been fun if I had been able to close the pages after a few hours. But it wasn't a novel. It was my life, a real life, and there was a lot more to it than nice cars, exotic locales and a lover who, I began to realize, was without a moral rudder.

There are a multitude of perspectives on just what I was doing in Southeast Asia and on what my life was like there.

From one perspective it is the story of a woman who makes a man an object of religious veneration and is hurt and wounded to discover that he is amoral except for the fact that he likes orchids. It is my story to be sure.

From another perspective it is the story of the life of a single-minded woman photographer who reads the Bible and uses its attitudes and words to inform her work. It would have me tripping along through the jungle, on the back of a motorcycle, saving souls through some oblique connection between light and time. Perhaps I would, on my missionary travels, find the Truth about Life. I would develop new relationships with my children, learn more about almost everything than I ever thought it possible to know and rediscover what I already knew—that home was the dearest spot on earth.

It could be a story from a chauvinistic point of view. It could be a story about the activities of women and how they work and see things. It could be a story of my photographing women as living examples of ancient texts; about the fact that women foreign correspondents are better than men at their job, kinder to the people in whose country they live, are generally better citizens and yet still have the same exciting, drug-filled, buddy life that their male counterparts do. It could be about how little recognition they get for their work and how grateful they are when that work is finally acknowledged. There is no question that it would be one of the stories that I lived to the hilt in Asia.

Or, it could be about how I thought one day I was becoming a butterfly. It would begin in the cocoon of a moth and it would follow the process of unraveling thought until—just at the very moment the self was about to merge into the bodiless and Unknown All—the words of the

Psalmist spoke to me and said, *Yea, though I walk through the valley of the shadow of death, I will fear no evil: for thou art with me. I will dwell in the house of the Lord forever.*

The story could be from the perspective of an American woman rooted in the decade of the fifties who, with more than three strikes against her and not playing with a full deck, nevertheless finds a mature self. I suppose that story is as true as any of the others.

If I had to give a last minute warning to a woman who was on her way to live such stories I would say, take your blanket, a short-wave radio, write home once a week and never, never for a moment forget who you are. Don't mistake being in love with a country with being in love with a man. Say your prayers.

Essentially I went to find myself and I did. I found that I changed what I saw that I didn't like into something else—something I liked better. I changed people's lives and they changed mine and none of us are the same as we were before our exchanges. I lived an adventurous, perilous life. Days, months, and eventually years were spent wandering on my own through the jungles, rice fields, markets and streets of the capitals of Asia, the subcontinent and Europe.

I read a library full of books, did a book of photographs and generally made myself at home under tropical and war-torn skies. There were some nice things about the times and the countries where I lived. There were some funny things and unforgettable things. Some history was made, some forgotten. I lived life as fully, though not as abundantly as I could. My children may or may not have suffered from the experience; we talked about it, and all we could conclude was that it was an unforgettable time. It's no overstatement to say that it could take a volume to describe the life I led during the four years I lived in Hong Kong, Manila and Bangkok, but I have only one story to tell.

CHAPTER 8

Bangkok

PRINCIPALITIES AND POWERS

FROM MY FIRST day in Bangkok, I heard screaming.

It pierced through the sounds of the city, the traffic, the people on the streets, the hum of air conditioners. The screaming was at another level, through some other sense, an inner ear.

"What is it?" I said to my colleague the first hour, in the elevator on the way up to the news bureau where I was to check in, on assignment to photograph the latest Prime Minister installed by the latest coup. What is it?

The wire service reporter who had lived in Bangkok for the past three years knew just what I meant.

"Don't ask," he said. "Don't ask."

But I did ask. There were no answers. The screaming did not go away. I could not sleep. Other people seemed not to hear. No one would discuss the fact that there was unbridled killing going on a little over 100 miles away.

Now a year after I went to China, after months in the Philippines, I lived in Bangkok, upstairs, in the first house past the gate at the end of Soi Kasem San 2, in a compound filled with thirty-nine varieties of tropical plants, nine of them orchids. Gene lived downstairs. He was covering Thai economic development for his business newspaper.

I had told a friend that I wanted to go as far into Cambodia as I could. He was a triple agent and a drug dealer. He was an American, his wife Vietnamese, a fragile-looking young woman in her twenties who kept her own stash of dope and a pistol on her side of the bed. He arranged for a captain in the Thai army to drive me to the border. Gene, along with most of his American male colleagues, said that he would have nothing to do with this investigation.

Along with hundreds of millions of others in the world he spoke out of classic denial—There Was Absolutely Nothing There. He said the screaming I heard night and day was in my mind, if I died I deserved it, he would not be surprised and he would certainly do nothing to lessen my children's grief. I believed the last part.

He was unprepared for adversity, afraid to go on assignment outside press conferences. I had packed him peanut butter sandwiches, given him Willie Nelson tapes and the down comforter I had brought to Asia as a protection against the air conditioning just to send him off with a car and driver to some tepid assignment.

Viewing me at first as an asset, then as competition, then as his own guilty conscience, he found I was nothing but a problem to him. It was a problem that I wouldn't let the maids serve food on their hands and knees in the Thai tradition. It was a problem when I went to church on Sundays rather than sit in the shade and watch him tend the orchids. Then there was the problem of the press conference we both attended.

I'd been hired by a Thai newspaper to coach its staff of twelve male photographers. One young photographer, arriving late for the first appearance of a Khmer Rouge leader since their takeover of Cambodia, caught a glimpse of Ieng Sary as he exited an elevator at the Oriental Hotel.

"I've got to get his autograph," said the young photographer, handing a pad of paper to Sary as he passed us.

"We don't get autographs from mass murderers," I said, taking the paper from Sary's hand.

"Crazy woman," said Sary as he passed in his gray Mao suit and entered the main hall where the press waited expectantly.

Gene cast me a fierce look. "Why are you always embarrassing me?" he asked.

*　　*　　*

It was still dark when the Thai army captain pulled his jeep into the driveway at 4 A.M. I carried my cameras and a book by Lillian Hellman in my sack to ease me into my culture again on the bus trip back. Gene didn't get up to say goodbye. As we drove out of Bangkok, the captain filled me in on the condition of the roads, the current political situation. We drove into the countryside and stopped at the end of some tire tracks to pick up a dead body in a small village, and, as the corpse bounced along behind me in the jeep, I was told the corpse had been an informer. We stopped off the roads and talked to villagers and by the time the sun came up, the mountains were in front of us, green and cool and dark.

I got out of the jeep and remembered China, the rock, the quiet of the rice fields. I saw men, moving so slowly they appeared to be tree stumps along the road. With fragments of clothes on and no shoes and no light in their eyes, they walked by me.

I found a refugee camp and, after asking permission in halting Thai or French, began to photograph each person alone or with their families, working silently with my 2¼ box camera. I did this work the way that I had a few years earlier in Washington, the way I had with children and women in the Philippines.

I had the stamina to photograph only three hundred fifty

people. Standing in the midst of a patch of dusty ground at the edge of the killing fields, I recorded men and women and children in their deepest agony.

As the light fell, near the barbed wire fence that kept refugees in limbo, two Western men, standing ten feet away, stared accusingly.

In the half-light of the evening on the Thai-Cambodian border I heard their unspoken question.

"Who is she and what is she doing here?"

And in the silence the spell that had kept me in Asia with Gene broke. Naivete, fear, foolishness, lack of self-definition—whatever had drawn me to first my husband, and then this man, to me or me to them—dissolved. I identified myself silently by name and added, without moving my lips, "I photograph."

I don't know how long I stood there in that circle of dust. But gathering myself together I walked down the road to the thatched hut where I had agreed to meet the army captain. He was sitting there drinking a Coke.

Exhausted I plunked down on a wooden stool and ordered a sugary tea, served in a small glass.

Gene was gone when I came back. I went downstairs, where the air conditioning was, to listen to music, rest, read the Bible, tried to get the dust off my feet.

When he came in, he stood in the middle of the room.

He had just returned from a party at the Oriental Hotel for women golfers from the United States. Wearing his blue orlon Highlands Golf Club sweater in the heat of Bangkok was really taking the extra step to dress for the occasion.

He described his attraction to the women and theirs to him, pacing back and forth across the room, looking down every now and then to see if I was still sitting on the sofa, whether I was jealous yet. Jealous? My mind was on the emotionally and physically starving human beings I had encountered on the dusty border, and he was parading a pretense of masculinity.

Had I raised my voice and told him that people were dying next door and a few miles away and that this assignment was not about sex or us or him, he would have accused me of having my period or being overly imaginative.

Even autogenocide within driving distance couldn't wake him from his dream. I had learned my lesson the hard way— through experience as a tourist in other people's realities.

"What's wrong?" he asked, sitting down next to me and throwing his head on my lap. Numbly, I picked up the Bible, opened it at random, and began reading out loud a letter from Paul.

For we wrestle not against flesh and blood but against princi-palities, against powers, against the rulers of darkness of this world, against spiritual wickedness in high places.

I was not, like Paul, whose insight overtook me, in Rome addressing a letter to the Ephesians. I was, however, caught in the crossfire of principalities, powers, rulers of darkness, spiritual wickedness in high places.

I had gone to Asia to be with the man I would spend my life with—so we had agreed years before in Hong Kong. What I had done, instead, was to use the gift I had, the camera, to define objectively the Cambodian men, women and children who escaped from the nameless indiscriminate chimerical death rained on them shortly after United States bombs had dropped on their country; to bring back, if I could, physical evidence that terrible things were happening. What I had done was to find myself in service of an idea.

I was not, nor had I ever been, a passionate defender of the faith, an observant, high-minded religionist, zealously articulating a vision. Up to my hips in adventure and competence, in over my head as a foreign correspondent with children, I had lived a very mixed life and wasn't all that keen about it.

Forgetting myself in the plights of the Cambodians, where before I heard screaming, I heard my name spoken. Words from the Bible that had seemed abstract, pronouncements from another time, were suddenly on the mark, more up to date than any newspaper account.

Trusting Paul, I could see that the difference between me

and Gene was not about merely whims and desires, frivolity and estrangement, foreigners or strangers; not only about the bottomless pool of practice and profession but about leaving my first love: intimacy with spiritual reasoning. The ties that had bound me to the dark side of this adventure were severed. Like Paul, I was free born. I left Gene.

I would make more trips to the border, bringing pictures of refugees to both Asian and Western publications and taking pictures back to people in the camps. Vietnam would invade Cambodia. Wholesale autogenocide stopped.

Although it was not politically correct at the time to hail the Vietnamese, their invasion of Cambodia was surely the lesser of the political and moral evils. Sometimes the lesser evil is all there is of good.

I had enlarged the borders of my tent. But what to do with what was inside the tent was now inescapable.

Shake thyself from the dust; arise and sit down, O Jerusalem: loose thyself from the bands of thy neck, O captive daughter of Zion.

San Francisco

MARY OF MAGDALA

WHEN I RETURNED to the States at the very end of the seventies, friends of Gene's, David and Jane, invited me to come and stay for a while.

"You will need some time," Jane said in a letter she had sent. "Come and go to the opera with us."

What she meant was that they would nurture me, love me, help me readjust and resettle. I had never heard of culture shock. They had. I had not looked at myself in a full-length mirror for years, not since the night in a Hong Kong hotel room when, torn by conflict, full of recognition that I was not myself, I had thrown a hairbrush at my reflection in the mirror. David and Jane saw how thin I was.

That's how I came to be sitting, spent, in an arm chair on the third floor of their house overlooking the Presidio in

San Francisco around three o'clock one afternoon reading the Bible, and listening to the sound of running water washing film in the darkroom across the study.

I had some questions that needed answering and picked up the telephone at my feet to call a friend who knew women, knew me, knew men, knew the Bible.

I asked him directly, "Why? What is that feeling I have that overwhelms me, what is it, that I don't know? Is it just middle age, culture shock or maybe," I said hopefully, "jet lag?"

"Turn to Luke 7:36," my friend said in that sonorous and sure tone of voice Bible believers sometimes get. I had called him, he hadn't called me. I turned.

And for yet another time I looked at Luke's story of the unnamed woman. It didn't look at all the same as it had when I pondered it some years before in Washington.

The woman was a still a scene stealer. But now I looked at the story not just from the emotional perspective of the weeping woman.

In the high-ceilinged room with the whitewashed walls, all eyes but those of Jesus were riveted on the woman and her actions.

The woman with the alabaster box of ointment stood behind his feet, weeping, washing his feet with tears, wiping them with her hair, kissing them, anointing them with oil.

Now when the Pharisee which had bidden him saw it, he spake within himself, saying, This man, if he were a prophet, would have known who and what manner of woman this is that toucheth him; for she is a sinner.

This was, it seemed, an all-male dinner party until the woman entered the scene. And not just an all-male dinner, but a meal in which hierarchy is clearly established. *The Pharisee had bidden.* This pharisaical consciousness is not identified by name but by rank and belief system. This consciousness "knows" automatically as part of an unequivocal history of being a male chosen by other males.

The Pharisee "saw" the woman's actions. As part of the dominant structure he does not presume that her actions are authentic. Nor does he presume that he is seen. He judges Jesus as men often judge other men—through the company of women they keep.

I could also see from the next passage that Jesus read the Pharisee's mind.

And Jesus answering said unto him, Simon, calling him by name, *I have somewhat to say unto thee. And he saith, Master, say on.*

Jesus talks in terms of money, the language of worth in which Nathan the prophet spoke to David about Bathsheba centuries before, the language that men often use to make their point.

A certain creditor, Jesus says, *had two debtors.* One of these debtors owed ten times more than the other but when the creditor saw that neither could pay, he wisely forgave them both their debt.

Tell me, therefore, says Jesus, *which will love him most?*

I suppose, Simon responds, *that he, to whom he forgave most. And he said unto him, Thou hast rightly judged. And he turned to the woman, and said unto Simon, Seest thou this woman?*

"Why did Jesus say, 'Seest thou this woman?' " said my friend who had been waiting as I found the page and read the first verses. "Simon had already seen her."

I had never asked myself that question.

"He didn't see her?" I said tentatively.

"Look at what Jesus, what the story has to say."

I entered into thine house, thou gavest me no water for my feet: but she hath washed my feet with tears, and wiped them with the hairs of her head.

Thou gavest me no kiss: but this woman since the time I came in hath not ceased to kiss my feet.

My head with oil thou did not anoint: but this woman hath anointed my feet with ointment.

Her sins, which are many, are forgiven; for she loved much.

My friend elaborated. "Jesus sees and retells her actions. He casts them in the light of Love forgiven by Love. It wasn't the woman who was wrong. It was the man.

"Most men," he added, "don't have the foggiest idea who women are or what they are doing. And I am a man. I speak from experience."

And then he asked me a second question.

"What does that story have to do with you?"

Well.

I had been seen as a sex object, I knew that much.

Something deeper was at work here. It was not obvious discrimination, not unequal pay for equal work, not sexual bargaining, not even that Jesus loves everybody. What was at issue in our dialogue about Simon, the woman and Jesus?

"The biggest problem," said my guide through this reading of Luke, "is that women believe the men's version of who and what they are. They take it personally and think it is their fault, that they did something wrong. Some women get sick because they are not appreciated, some get desperate, some go from man to man, some die without ever being recognized for their selfless love. Women, and the world, suffer from sexism."

The Bible, an exposé of sexism?

This was the kind of thinking that ran counter to all popular belief. It had the ring of truth to me.

I stopped.

The Bible reported how men treated women. Reporting is not necessarily approval. No longer did I see the unnamed woman as a literal and shortened reading of the text that describes her; a sinner forgiven because she loved Jesus. I saw her, this moment, as a catalyst exposing the kind of blind, unthinking, animalistic hatred so deep, so horrendous, so much a part of the very retina upon which I saw my female identity that I cradled the phone between my shoulder and ear and folded my hands in sorrow.

I saw psychic and physical death by category; biblically described by orders from Pharoah, Herod to kill all newborn males. Categorical death that slays all foreigners within the borders, or, all women or newborn females. The kind of death I had seen in Cambodia.

The Pharisees at dinner that night saw their own shortcomings as woman, who to them was a category, not an individual. It was Eve they saw. Woman, the same, whatever the place or time.

"Look at it this way," my friend on the phone continued. "Men project their lust on women and then women get confused. This woman Luke describes didn't get confused. She knew what she was doing."

One last question.

"When you were in Asia, did you love?"

Did I love?

Oh, Lord.

It was a question that silenced.

Speculative theology stops at that question.

When did I love? Who did I love, where, what, when and why did I, if I did at all, Love?

I made a list.

When I was a child, like most all children, I loved everybody in my family.

I loved Gwendolyn.

Later, I loved my children.

My grandmother.

Easy; I was a woman at the cusp of the "me decade."

There were the children in the Philippines, the class I adopted and clothed and bathed and fed and gave parties for during the nine months I lived in Manila.

There were the refugees and the Thai maids who I wouldn't allow to serve on their knees, the Muslim woman whose husband I helped bury, whose children I helped educate.

So. I could put myself in some other people's places. So?

But then, there was the poetry of basketball, the Seattle Supersonics, Bill Russell, K.C. Jones, Dr. J., the Celtics, Bulls, Knicks.

Didn't I have anything else to do but to track the NBA?

Geraniums, the smell of verbena, the taste of lemon-grass.

The list was unveiling me, giving me shape, defining me.

Fast cars, good socks, enforceable contracts.

Hot bread.

Beaujolais Nouveau for Thanksgiving.

Singular moments.

The harder list. Loving that no one but the lover knows anything about, and no one but the lover knows the cost. Loving that is so natural that the lover doesn't think about it as love but as the very substance of Life. Self-sacrifice, self-forgetfulness. In others more than in myself.

Who was this self-forgetful, unnamed woman with the long hair and tears, at an otherwise all-male dinner party, a woman, dead two thousand years, informing my life and my work, living there, here in the shadows of my mind, my unseen being?

Theologians to date, and in their wake the world, have presumed the unnamed woman to be Mary Magdalene. The Bible doesn't say that the woman Luke records who washed Jesus' feet at the Pharisee's dinner was Mary Magdalene, but as all women look alike to some men, most popular belief assumes the two women to be one. And as there are several Gospel stories of women anointing Jesus, they have often been lumped together.

Now a certain man was sick, named Lazarus, of Bethany, the town of Mary and her sister Martha. (It was that Mary which anointed the Lord with ointment, and wiped his feet with her hair, whose brother Lazarus was sick.), says John in the eleventh chapter of his recounting. But oddly enough it is not until the twelfth chapter that John tells the story that takes place in Mary's house; her sister Martha serves the meal, the house is filled with *the odour of the ointment.*

Mark tells of an unnamed woman in Bethany who came with an alabaster box of ointment at the house of Simon the leper. In these stories of women anointing amidst male disapproval, the men don't see what is going on. The point is illustrated again when Jesus washes his disciples' feet at the Passover supper before his crucifixion.

What I do thou knowest not now; but thou shalt know here-after.

Peter saith unto him, Thou shalt never wash my feet. Jesus answered him, If I wash thee not, thou hast no part with me.

And after Jesus finishes washing all the disciples' feet he says, *Ye call me Master and Lord: and ye say well; for so I am. If I then, your Lord and Master, have washed your feet; ye also ought to wash one another's feet.*

For I have given you an example, that ye should do as I have done to you.

Mary of Magdala's life, what is known of it, is found in little more than a handful of references in the gospels of Matthew, Mark, Luke and John. It can be pieced together, like most lives, only from fragments.

Nowhere in any of these references is she identified as a prostitute. Mary Magdalene *is* reported as one of the ministers who accompanies Jesus on several trips. Mark describes Mary as *the woman out of whom Jesus cast several devils,* but that is not surprising, as the theme of his report is casting out demons.

Matthew, Mark and John report that Mary Magdalene stood with Mary, the mother of Jesus, at the foot of the cross through the crucifixion.

Mary went to the tomb on the third day and discovered the stone rolled away from the sepulchre. Depending on whose gospel version is read, she heard a voice or saw a man who told her to tell the disciples. Matthew has the "other" Mary with the Magdalene. The women were on their way to tell the disciples when they saw Jesus, fell at his feet, held them. He told them to not be afraid.

Mark says Jesus appeared to Mary Magdalene *the first day of the week,* and that her report was not believed. Luke has Mary, the mother of James and Salome, hearing the news that Jesus was not in the tomb and their report received as *idle tales.* John records that Mary Magdalene saw the stone rolled away from the sepulchre and that she ran to tell Peter and *the other disciple, whom Jesus loved*—presumably John himself.

Mary, John and Peter ran to the tomb. John arrived before Peter. The men looked in, saw the linen wrappings, and, *For as yet they knew not the scripture, that he must rise again from the dead,* went home.

Mary stayed there.

She stood outside the sepulchre weeping and as she wept she stooped down and looked yet again into the sepulchre. Through her tears she saw two angels who talked with her.

Woman, why weepest thou? they asked her.

She answers, *Because they have taken away my Lord, and I know not where they have laid him.*

She turned herself back, and saw Jesus standing, and knew not that it was Jesus.

He asks her what the angels asked her. *Woman, why weepest thou?* and further, *whom seekest thou?*

She supposing him to be the gardener, saith unto him, Sir, if thou have borne him hence, tell me where thou hast laid him, and I will take him away.

Jesus saith unto her, Mary.

She turned herself, and saith unto him, Rabboni; which is to say, Master.

Jesus saith unto her, Touch me not; for I am not yet ascended to my Father: but go to my brethren, and say unto them, I ascend unto my Father and your Father; and to my God, and your God.

A man who would say that he was in the process of Ascension, who had actually been seen to walk on water, to appear and disappear at will, to willingly suffer and survive public crucifixion chose to have a woman carry his message. A man able to move his physical self through time and space is not a man to be taken lightly, not a man who overlooks details. He could have chosen anyone, but chose her, a woman.

If you've been chosen or misunderstood, you experience what Mary Magdalene experienced. If you are at the right place, at the right time, then you are following in the footsteps of the Magdalene. If you've ever been a woman alone—with and then without a good man in your life—you know what it's like to be Mary Magdalene.

All biblical accounts of Mary Magdalene's life say that except for Jesus, men misunderstood her. Her reports were not believed, even though the actual arm of the Lord had been revealed to her. She was in the right place at the right time. She saw something no one else did and she reported it. Her report of the Resurrection wasn't believed. There is, to be sure, a little bit of her in all of us.

Mary became a pawn in the religious dialectic. She became known as a sinning woman forgiven by the Lord. In fact, she was an active minister and first at the tomb.

Is she, was she, a real woman? Or just a figure of woman put there to make a point about men, fleshed out to suit a variety of interpretations?

Luke records in the book of Acts that eleven men, *with the women, and Mary the mother of Jesus, and with his brethren* were meeting in an upper room in Jerusalem—all of one accord in prayer and supplication. It is more than possible Mary of Magdala was one of the women there on the day of Pentecost, filled with the Holy Ghost as the Spirit gave her utterance—just as countless unnamed and historically named women of today are watching, listening, reporting and witnessing.

CHAPTER 10

Paris

THE KING'S DAUGHTER

CULTURE SHOCK DID hit me over the next four years. After years of shopping daily for fresh food in the stalls of Asian streets, bargaining for mangoes, pineapples and beans, the supermarkets with food wrapped in plastic, fluorescent lights and piped in sounds imitating music seemed to me soulless halls of impersonal overchoice. When people asked me what I had been doing and I mentioned Cambodia, they would turn away.

My daughter graduated from college, and I took her on a trip through Europe. One afternoon over tea and tarts at Fauchon's we decided to move to France. Despite the tea and tarts, it was not a frivolous decision. I was deeply disquieted by the direction my own country was taking. Self-imposed exile seemed the way to go.

For my daughter it was an appropriate postcollege year.

Kristin found work as a model. Tom decided college wasn't for him and, leaving school, joined us. In Paris we had an apartment in the shadow of the Eiffel Tower. I had time to sit by the fire in an armchair and read. It was a sabbatical for my soul.

The French as a rule take pride in work well done, in a certain sense of the way things should be. And few things pleased me more than shopping early each evening for fresh fruits, meats, fish, vegetables, wine and bread. At the dinner table, where my children and guests and I lit candles, we ate slowly and with relish while we carried on conversations where common issues were in the air, thoughts sustained themselves long enough to find form and no one was at fault for expressing themselves.

I took long, leisurely lunches with a woman banker, dropped into the fashion houses for a seasonal new dress, went to church regularly, found a flower stand whose owner pushed purple, red, blue, white and orange blooms into my waiting hands, set the radio to the station whose music charmed and educated me into the best of past and present Western tones. Monday noon Kristin and I would meet at the drugstore at the base of the Arc de Triomphe to pick up the Sunday *New York Times,* reading yesterday's news over a hamburger and *frites.*

Paris, a city so sure of itself, so insistent on being looked at, so used to refugees from the crumbled French foreign policy in Southeast Asia, was entirely unimpressed, unmoved by the fact that one more woman dwelled in its embrace.

There were long, lazy days, opened by a walk to the corner for fresh bread, croissants and the *International Herald Tribune.* Kristin would make coffee and steam milk. Sitting at the kitchen table we would talk about politics, about the economy, and on one particular day, about children.

"France would be a great place to have children," she said. "The clothes are so adorable. I can just see us pushing strollers in the Jardin du Luxembourg."

Kristin and I were as close as any two women, or any mother and daughter, would ever hope to be. But for the past decade there was one area in which our points of view clearly diverged. She thought all things were not only possible but her right. Our upbringings were very different. I thought all things were possible, but not necessarily my right. And one thing I didn't think was a right was to have a child because the children's clothes in France were adorable.

At fourteen she had thought she would grow up to marry the son of the Shah of Iran. I thought that was not only pretentious but improbable. It had been two decades since those days when the women who lived in the suburbs where I grew up had no other model but marriage. My daughter had a mother who spent years working in Asia and a father she did not know.

Visitors came and went, some staying for dinner, some for a few weeks. Between concerts, strolls in the Tuileries, hours at the bookstores, an occasional photography assignment, I had time to revisit the women of the Bible. One evening, I was drawn to a reference to the King's daughter.

The king's daughter is all glorious within.

Given my contentment, the sense of dominion I had over my life, and the freedom I had from denominational constrictions, this woman fascinated me. I searched the Scriptures for her. I found her from the first chapter to the last.

The King's daughter is the woman of First Genesis, the female of *male and female created he them.* All the promises of dominion echoed throughout the Bible apply to her.

And thou, O tower of the flock, the stronghold of the daughter of Zion, unto thee shall it come, even the first dominion; the kingdom shall come to the daughter of Jerusalem.

She has never known anything but the Divine Love bestowed upon her before and since her birth.

Before I formed thee in the belly I knew thee; and before thou camest forth out of the womb I sanctified thee.

The King's daughter draws her wisdom and her trust, her strength, from God's Word.

Fear thou not; for I am with thee: be not dismayed; for I am thy God: I will strengthen thee; yea, I will help thee: yea, I will uphold thee with the right hand of my righteousness.

So shall my word be that goeth forth out of my mouth: it shall not return unto me void, but it shall accomplish that which I please, and it shall prosper in the thing whereto I sent it.

She is wise enough to know that her Father-Mother loves her and she is in awe of the kingdom They have given her.

God is love; and he that dwelleth in love dwelleth in God, and God in him.

Princes have persecuted me without a cause: but my heart standeth in awe of they word.

The King's daughter is a Representative of the Kingdom. She takes, as gifts to strangers and to friends, the first fruits of the Kingdom.

For all the law is fulfilled in one word, even in this; Thou shalt love thy neighbor as thyself.

The King's daughter has her clearly defined place. She plays in the snow, walks by the sea, climbs the mountains of her country in peace and in absolute secure knowledge that she owns these lands—prepared and waiting for her under any circumstances.

Hast thou entered into the treasures of the snow? or hast thou seen the treasures of the hail, Which I have reserved against the time of trouble, against the day of battle and war?

She rests, when she chooses, by still waters.

Knowing who she is makes her the more appreciative of those who treat her as a real woman and not as a symbol.

Seest thou this woman?

How fair is thy love, my sister, my spouse! How much better is thy love than wine! and the smell of thine ointments than all spices!

The King's daughter is a welcome participant in government and in the business of her Parent's kingdom. She is occupied in the raising of children, the arts, education, shipping, commerce and has legions of warriors at her command.

Now gather thyself in troops. O daughter of troops.

They that go down to the sea in ships, that do business in great waters; These see the works of the Lord, and his wonders in the deep.

And kings shall be thy nursing fathers, and their queens thy nursing mothers;

The Lord recompense thy work, and a full reward be given thee of the Lord God of Israel, under whose wings thou art come to trust.

And there appeared a great wonder in heaven; a woman clothed with the sun, and the moon under her feet, and upon her head a crown of twelve stars.

The King's daughter is not Eve.

CHAPTER 11

Santa Fe

THE VIRTUOUS WOMAN

MANY PEOPLE, WHEN thinking of Santa Fe, think of the desert. Those who have been there or who have looked at topographical maps know, in fact, that the city lies in the high desert and that the environs are green. Every few years or so the winter is mild with little or no skiing, but I remember one winter when the pipes froze in April at 22 degrees below zero Fahrenheit and the airport in Albuquerque, sixty miles away and three thousand feet down the mountains, was closed for three days by snow.

Driving up to Santa Fe from Albuquerque one sees signs marking the exits to the Indian reservations, Los Alamos to the left and, as the road levels off at La Bajada Hill, Santa Fe lies in the distance at the foot of the Sangre de Cristo Mountains. The red light of sunset on the mountains caused the Spanish *conquistadores* to name them for the blood of Christ, and the Spanish thought that the gold leaves of the aspens in the fall was gold ore lying on the mountains to be picked up and harvested by hand.

The Spaniards were the first Judeo-Christians in the land and they left their mark on the names of the places and on the consciousness of their descendants.

One moves off the plateaus down the hill and to the edge of town where malls and fast-food chains give evidence that the culture is being crowded in from the outside. Close up, in the center of town off the plaza, there remain picturesque streets lined with pine trees, aspens and elms, and lilacs and peach trees and orchards and cactus and adobe walls behind which, one thinks, lie many secrets.

The scenery, if physical perfection can be called scenery, is best experienced first hand, over a long period of time. This is a truth about Santa Fe. This is a truth about anything or any relationship that is valuable and important as well as a truth about Santa Fe. There is no city quite like it anywhere in the world although at Christmas only the absence of armed soldiers visually distinguishes the city's earth-colored buildings and narrow candle-lit streets from Bethlehem.

The light in the sky or the smell of the place led men and women to choose this place above all others. The big city, Los Angeles or New York they say, is so rootless, so new, so full of evil.

Depending on one's perspective I found my home in

Santa Fe either because I had a lot of cash and an aggressive realtor, or because I repeated the 23rd Psalm so many times during the fours years I spent covering politics and war in China and Southeast Asia.

In my Father's house are many mansions; if it were not so, I would have told you. I go to prepare a place for you.

In any event what came true in my early forties, when in a mirror of the national mood, I was no longer wanting and thought I was in no danger, I found a house that came with green pastures and a river.

For some years I'd owned land a few miles out of Santa Fe in the Tesuque valley. On summer nights, the strains of *Don Giovanni* or the *Marriage of Figaro* could be heard streaming down the hills from the Santa Fe Opera. I thought often of the property when I was in Bangkok and on the Cambodian border. I dreamed sometimes of building a house there, a tower, where like Rapunzel I could let down my hair, where I could see for miles unobstructed by palm trees and wars and mutilated children and men and women.

When I went back to northern New Mexico to make my dream a reality, I found that four men with BMW 733s and no visible means of support had filled the valley with horses, drugs, Indian artifacts and young, wide-eyed women who lived in their dream. I sold them the land and called a realtor.

On the third day she showed me the property of a Scandinavian woman. The floors of the house were linoleum, the beams were not telephone poles but square and light. There was a bidet and the house was decidedly European. But it was the meadow, the river and the trees that captivated me. The owner wanted me to have it. I was the only woman who looked at the house who had not brought in a decorator to change the linoleum. And, I am Scandinavian.

After I owned the house for some time, I learned that the former owner, the widow of the man who had built the house, was the sister-in-law of Greta Garbo. It wasn't until later that neighbors told me Garbo had been sighted in a boat in the meadow during the summer that the river had overflowed its banks and made a pond out of the pasture.

Naturally I went through an intensely Greta Garbo phase, staring out the window at the apricot tree blossoming in the spring sun and wind of the Cerro Gordo valley.

Both in the world and out of it, I had, for a time, dropped out of work, social engagements and been quietly living my life, taking care of daily details, reading the Bible and every other book that passed my way.

I had no particular problems, no consuming passions, no

plan but to enjoy my days when I realized that through some foresight and a moderate inheritance, I owned several valuable pieces of real estate and a small portfolio of stocks. Ten per cent of my cash assets were in silver and gold in a Zurich bank account. Healthy, grown children, an eclectic wardrobe, and scented candles in each of three bathrooms rounded out a short list of my assets.

Doing it all, a list of my financial assets in front of me for the Internal Revenue Service, I said to Kristin as we were sitting in what I still thought of as Garbo's bedroom, "I ought to be a corporation."

"How will you explain this idea to a lawyer?" she asked, now very tired of repeating the line about working it out for eternity.

The candles started me thinking. I went into the bathroom and looked at the flickering flame of one white candle and thought of the verse: *She perceiveth that her merchandise is good: her candle goeth not out by night.*

I wanted to know what the rest of the poem said, the way one does when bits of poetry or song drift through memory. Instinct told me that the words held the answer to Kristin's question, the answer to the self-definition I was looking for.

I put away the list of assets, and looked in the Bible for the other twenty-one verses of the poem in Proverbs 31— wisdom attributed to Solomon.

I read, *Who can find a virtuous woman? for her price is far above rubies*, through verses of the poem that enumerate the assets of a superwoman in the time of the patriarchs.

The heart of her husband doth safely trust in her, so that he shall have no need of spoil.

She will do him good and not evil all the days of her life.

She seeketh wool, and flax, and worketh willingly with her hands. She is like the merchants' ships; she bringeth her food from afar.

She riseth also while it is yet night, and giveth meat to her household, and a portion to her maidens.

She considereth a field and buyeth it: with the fruit of her hands she planteth a vineyard.

She girdeth her loins with strength and strengtheneth her arms.

She perceiveth that her merchandise is good: her candle goeth not out by night.

She layeth her hands to the spindle, and her hands hold the distaff.

She stretcheth out her hand to the poor; yea she reacheth forth her hands to the needy.

She is not afraid of the snow for her household: for all her household are clothed with scarlet.

She maketh herself coverings of tapestry; her clothing is silk and purple.

Her husband is known in the gates, when he sitteth among the elders of the land.

She maketh fine linen, and selleth it; and delivereth girdles unto the merchant.

Strength and honour are her clothing; and she shall rejoice in time to come.

She openeth her mouth with wisdom; and in her tongue is the law of kindness.

She looketh well to the ways of her household, and eateth not the bread of idleness.

Her children arise up, and call her blessed; her husband also, and he praiseth her.

Many daughters have done virtuously, but thou excellest them all.

Favour is deceitful, and beauty is vain: but a woman that feareth the Lord, she shall be praised.

Give her of the fruit of her hands; and let her own works praise her in the gates.

I looked at that forty-nine-cent candle that I had bought and lit, thinking, I am a woman, that woman.

I had heard that the poem was about the subjugation of women through idealization. I had heard that it was about Israel. I had heard that it was a mystical expression of Christ's relation to the Church. But once more, it was my life that seemed clarified by this biblical description of woman.

Is it only Americans who can't deal with paradox and who take everything personally? I had no husband. But for that, I thought, the words described me. I was terrified. Had it come to this? Fitting Bible phrases to a context that they didn't fit? Did it mean that God was my husband, as Isaiah had said?

Parallels hadn't bothered me when I was in trouble. Why should they startle me when there was no trouble?

Did this mean, I wondered, that I had done all a woman could do?

Should I enter a convent?

Which convent?

Who would have me with the religious beliefs that I held? I was convinced that women were not necessarily religious but that because they were powerless in this world, God, the God of the Bible at least, regularly visited them, good, bad and even, obviously, apparently otherwise occupied.

And so, instead of looking more deeply into the text, instead of rejoicing in the abundance of the impartial and impersonal activities of Spirit, instead of remembering Isaiah and that everyone who thirsteth can come to the waters, I dismissed the episode, reminding myself there were many ways to read a text. As do many Bible readers, I missed the spacious, more meaty elements involved in the spiritual meaning of finding, of discovery, of jewels, of treasures, of gates and possible directions to the Holy City.

As a result, I spent most of that time in the American West as a contemporary cowgirl. I drove a fast BMW, played Emmy Lou Harris on the tape deck, drank Coors from a can. Proverbs didn't mention any of that.

CHAPTER 12

Santa Fe

$\mathcal{R}$UTH

THERE WAS SOMETHING I could not dismiss. Not sure what was swirling around my thought, looking for clarity, I left the kitchen and the dishes and went out into the sun on the deck overlooking the valley, where I stood expectantly, Bible in hand.

I found myself in the book of Ruth, in the presence of Naomi.

Marriage had changed Naomi's life. She left her home during a famine and followed her husband to Moab, a foreign country.

Moab was not simply a political territory. The Hebrew translation defines Moab as water, seed, progeny of a father.

Naomi's two sons married Ruth and Orpah, sisters they met there. By the fifth verse of the book of Ruth, the men have died and faded from the narrative.

The women are left alone with each other and with their options.

Naomi did not sit and bewail her fate.

Then she arose with her daughters in law, that she might return from the country of Moab: for she had heard in the country of Moab how that the Lord had visited his people in giving them bread.

I imagined her rising to her full height, her stature strong, and purposeful against the landscape.

The women could have stayed where they were, with the full expectation that they would be martyrs to the poverty of widowhood and barrenness. Or they could return to Naomi's maternal home, Bethlehem, where the famine had passed and *the Lord had visited his people.*

They were not fools. They were not chattels. They knew where to go.

They turned toward Bethlehem.

Somewhere along the way, the story doesn't say where, Naomi told the other two women to return, not to their father's house, but to their mother's house, with her blessing and hope that they will find rest, each in the house of her husband. Why Naomi waited until they were packed and had left home and were along the route is not clear. Perhaps that delay was the reason for their response.

And they said unto her, Surely we will return with thee unto thy people.

Turn again, my daughters, says Naomi, confronting them with her practicality in the face of tradition. *If I should have a husband tonight,* she says, *and should also bear sons, would you wait for them until they were grown?*

That long look down a husbandless future may be one reason Orpah kissed her mother-in-law, and went back to her people.

Ruth stayed.

For the third time Naomi told Ruth to go back.

There then occurs that brilliantly poetic response from Ruth, the statement that many people think a woman said to a man. In fact it is a woman-to-woman sentiment.

Intreat me not to leave thee, or to return from following after thee: for whither thou goest, I shall go; and where thou lodgest, I will lodge: thy people shall be my people, and thy God my God.

If I should say, I have hope: if I should have a husband also tonight, and should also bear sons, would ye tarry for them till they were grown?

It was not, I thought, that Ruth was the loyal one, as the story is often interpreted, but that she was the one who opted for a relationship with Naomi's God, the one visiting her mother-in-law's people.

What was it about this God that gave Ruth the idea that this was what she wanted? Was it Naomi's life? Had she seen evidence? I couldn't tell from the words on the page.

What I could tell was that Ruth was talking commitment.

Where thou diest, will I die, and there will I be buried: the Lord do so to me, and more also, if ought but death part thee and me.

When she saw that she was steadfastly minded to go with her, Naomi stopped talking.

Did Naomi know that two daughters-in-law with other gods would be complicated business in Bethlehem? Did she know that singular commitment would be needed for their future?

The two went until they come to Bethlehem. All the city said, *Is this Naomi?*

Her response was dramatic in its starkness and allusions. I could almost see her standing there, legs apart, feet planted firmly on the ground, hand over the dark hair falling onto her forehead, the center of attention of the whole city as the words, *Call me not Naomi, call me Mara: for the Almighty hath dealt very bitterly with me,* spit from her lips.

She looked forty or so to me.

Naomi's fellow citizens knew, as surely as they knew the name Naomi meant pleasantness, that the name Mara meant sadness. The name was a word play on Marah, the name of the bitter wells of water that the women who went through the parted sea to the promised land with Miriam and Aaron and Moses encountered just after following a pillar of fire and a cloud through the dry Sea.

It must have been a comedown to find bitter water after such an experience. The human mind always looks for the perfect, happy ending. The followers of Moses blamed him. Naomi, a direct woman, blamed the Almighty. She was bitter and didn't care who knew it.

I went out full, she said, *and the Lord hath brought me home again empty: why then call ye me Naomi, seeing the Lord hath testified against me, and the Almighty hath afflicted me?*

There was no answer from the crowd.

So Naomi returned, and Ruth the Moabitess, her daughter in law, with her, which returned out of the country of Moab: and they came to Bethlehem in the beginning of barley harvest.

The field in front of me where the Martinez family had harvested barley for the past seven decades sprouted clumps of grain here and there in the Santa Fe sun. It melted into the field where Ruth was about to glean.

And Naomi had a kinsman of her husband's, coincidentally *a mighty man of wealth,* of the family of Naomi's husband, Elimelech—"to whom God is King."

Of course Naomi and Ruth knew that the law in Israel required a husband's male relatives to marry his widow, to assume responsibility for his women. Of course they knew to go back to Bethlehem. There, in Bethlehem, if nothing else, was a mighty man of wealth, a relative of the house of those to whom God is King.

Of course Naomi made a scene in the town square and recounted in no uncertain terms that she had gone out full and come back empty. News traveled fast, and the male relatives had to be notified. Naomi and Ruth were not passive women, not mere instruments for patriarchy. They were women allied in the business of turning a barren situation into a very, very fruitful one.

And Ruth the Moabitess said unto Naomi, Let me now go to the field, and glean ears of corn after him in whose sight I shall find grace. And she said unto her, Go, my daughter.

Bitterness dissolved in activity. Opportunities presented themselves and were acted upon.

Ruth knew. I *shall,* she said, not "maybe." Not, "if I am lucky." I *shall,* find grace in the field. She was no more the daughter-in-law. She was the daughter, plain and simple.

And, of course, Boaz, Naomi's wealthy male relative, came to the field and saw Ruth and heard who she was.

He said, *The Lord recompense thy work, and a full reward be given thee of the Lord God of Israel, under whose wings thou art come to trust.*

Putting his money where his mouth was he gave Ruth room to glean in the fields and find her own food. He also gave her protection from the men who wanted to molest her.

I could almost hear the rustle of wings in the breeze blowing over the valley.

Ruth told Naomi what her employer, their hope, Boaz had said. Naomi, with wisdom and knowledge of the laws of Israel, set up the marital situation. Ruth followed

Naomi's suggestions, dressed up, lay at Boaz's feet all night, and left in the morning *before one could know another.*

Boaz gave her six measures of barley telling her, *Go not empty unto thy mother in law.*

Ruth related Boaz's words to Naomi who said with authority:

Sit still, my daughter, until you know how the matter will fall: for the man will not be in rest, until he have finished the thing this day.

Boaz dealt with the legal arrangements for the wedding.

So Boaz took Ruth, and she was his wife: and when he went in unto her; the Lord gave her conception, and she bare a son.

The women's mourning became joy, their empty lives spilled over with fullness, continuity, promise.

The women of the city said to Naomi, *Blessed be the Lord, which hath not left thee this day without a kinsman, that his name may be famous in Israel. And he shall be unto thee a restorer of thy life, and a nourisher of thine old age: for thy daughter in law, which loveth thee, which is better to thee than seven sons, hath born him.*

And Naomi took the child, and laid it in her bosom, and became nurse unto it.

And the women her neighbors gave it a name, saying, there is a son born to Naomi; and they called his name Obed: he is the father of Jesse, the father of David, poet-king and unifier of Israel.

Transported by the text to Bethlehem and the happy ending, I read the sequel to Ruth, which, in the King James Version of the Bible, is I Samuel.

The themes of the Book of Ruth were repeated.

But this time there was a husband in the picture—a man who did not understand his wife's desire. He wonders why his love for his wife isn't enough for her.

Am I not better to thee than ten sons? he asks.

Hannah rose up, after they had eaten in Shiloh, and took her stand before the Lord.

Hannah was an independent woman.

Eli, the priest, didn't see that, as he sat on a seat by a post in the temple, watching her weep.

She turns inward and prays silently to herself as she asks the Lord to give her a son—only her lips moved.

O Lord of hosts, if thou wilt indeed look on the affliction of thine handmaid, and remember me, and not forget thine handmaid, but will give unto thine handmaid a man child, then I will give him unto the Lord all the days of his life, and there shall no rasor come upon his head.

Instead of seeing a woman praying silently, what Eli saw, as he looked on, was a drunken spectacle.

How long will thou be drunken? put away thy wine from thee, he says.

And Hannah answered and said, No, my lord, I am a woman of a sorrowful spirit: I have drunk neither wine nor strong drink, but have poured out my soul before the Lord.

Out of the abundance of my complaint and grief have I spoken, she adds.

I read the story in some emotional place that was familiar territory, as familiar as the field in the sun in front of me.

Eli, corrected by Hannah, says, *Go in peace: and the God of Israel grant thee thy petition that thou hast asked of him.*

I dwelt with Hannah for a time before I turned back to the story.

So the woman went her way, and did eat, and her countenance was no more sad.

Hannah and Elkanah worship together, and after dinner at home, in Ramah where Rachel was heard weeping for her children, *Elkanah knew Hannah his wife; and the Lord remembered her.*

The Lord remembered her.

Elkanah knew his wife $=$ A.

The Lord remembered her $=$ B.

AB equals a son, Samuel.

The juxtaposition of the conjugal relationship and Divine causation seemed that afternoon with Ruth, Naomi and Hannah, as simple as basic math.

I saw something I hadn't expected to see: knowing made alive by remembering.

The product was a son, named by Hannah, Samuel, *Because I have asked him of the Lord.*

Gloriously, sparkling water gathered together into complex patterns danced in the clear light blue space over the valley. I gathered the idea of knowing and Divine remembrance under my arm with the Book as I walked back into the house and into the kitchen.

Over the sink and the dishes, I understood that what had been swirling around my thought was an unresolved difference between my attitude about abortion and my daughter's. She had taken the attitude, I thought, that an abortion was a deserved rite of passage.

Unresolved in my heart, I had been moved on to the deck

and into the Book of Ruth. The politically correct attitudes I thought I had taken in helping her, an adult of legal age, through the abortion, the pain I had suffered silently in my support for her to make her own choice, to continue, if she chose, the pregnancy and deliver a child, the deep pit in which I had apparently buried my feeling that she was dominated by a man, his mother and popular belief, all that, all that disappeared, swallowed up into the unseen—dissolved during the time I had dwelt with Naomi, Ruth and Hannah.

A year or so passed.

We had the family wedding on Jayne's boat on Lake Michigan with the Chicago skyline behind us. My stepmother, Jayne, had done everything along a nautical theme: organizing the men to wear blue blazers, making sure the lobster and champagne were chilled just so, the flowers crisp, fresh and fragrant.

The reception was a week later on my deck in Santa Fe. We played volleyball in the meadow in a spot where we had cleared the barley and set up a net. Kristin mingled with the hundred or more guests of all ages, visited quietly with people who had known her since childhood, giggled with her contemporaries, posed for pictures.

Kristin was pregnant and lovely, her brother and my

brother supportive, just as one wants brothers to be. All was as one wished it should be.

At Christmas my daughter gave birth to a son. I held Russell against my breast and for hours rocked him in welcome as Naomi must have rocked Obed.

Two years later his sister, Hannah, was born.

PART THREE

They have healed also the hurt of the daughter of my people slightly, saying, Peace, peace; when there is no peace.

JEREMIAH 6: 14

CHAPTER 13

Los Angeles—Santa Fe

$\mathcal{T}$HE MINISTERS

IMPECCABLY TAILORED, over six feet tall, the Reverend Doctor Billy Graham, bearing an uncanny resemblance to my father, swept into the library of his Los Angeles office. He raised his arm to shake my hand, saying, "William Randolph Hearst anointed me."

The occasion was the sixty-fifth birthday of the world's most prominent contemporary evangelist. As a syndicated columnist and the religion writer for the newspaper that first promoted him, I had been scheduled to interview him and add to the symmetry of his career.

A column of his a few years earlier had troubled me in its response to a woman who stated she had been married three times and, in her twenties, still felt she hadn't found happiness or comfort with a man. Graham, or whoever wrote the column under his name, had told the woman that she should accept Jesus as her personal saviour but hadn't said a word about what her husbands should, could or ought to do or have done.

Moving toward the issue of equality in marriage, I asked Dr. Graham about his position on women in the ministry.

"We don't have that problem in my denomination," he said. "I've heard women preach who were very good, but women don't have that role in our denomination."

I sighed.

In the past five years, I had interviewed over three thousand women, asking them what religion meant to them, how, where and why they and the world might be going in the area of women's religious beliefs.

How long was this business going to go on, I wondered. How long before there would be some *Seest thou this woman?* some recognition that millions upon hundreds of millions into the billions of women ministered, every hour, every day. Life itself was not denomination but ministry. Love itself, Life.

I'd gone back to the paper, written up the interview, waited for it to be edited and slotted for the next day's paper, gone back to the airport, flown to Albuquerque, stopped at the roadside inn before the freeway entrance to Santa Fe to pick up a barbecue sandwich and a beer for the drive home, thinking as the miles passed of the symmetry of my own career.

My house looked like an electric company ad when I pulled into the driveway. Every light in every window was on. My daughter, pregnant now with Hannah, was on the bed, Russell asleep at her feet; the television flickered with a sitcom.

"They called," she said. "Dad died. They want you to call them."

It never occurred to me to ask who called. I knew. I asked her how she was doing.

She said she wasn't at all affected. She turned back to the television while I dialed.

"My deepest sympathies," said the voice that I hadn't heard in twenty-five years. "He had a lot of markers out, but I told 'em all to get in line behind me, he was my friend."

They really do talk that way.

There had been two wives after me, but I was the one they asked about what to do with the body.

My children assured me this was a sign of respect.

I declined the offer of plane tickets for the children, called my brother to meet my daughter and Russ in Chicago, put them on a plane, took another one an hour later to New York to meet my son and give him his ticket to Chicago and the funeral. Somewhere over St. Louis I burst into uncontrollable sobbing, overcome by emotions bottled up for decades. Washing the tears from my face in the bathroom, I looked into the mirror. The realities of my life were not reflected in the image in the glass. There was no evidence on that image of the burden I felt leaving my body.

Later, after a long talk with the official historian of the Baptist church, I learned that by "denomination" Dr. Graham had meant his worldwide organization and not the Baptist church of which he was an ordained minister. The church historian gave me dozens of names of Baptist women through the past century who had served as ministers from the pulpit. "It's a problem," he said, "when a church has a hard time admitting its own history as far as women are concerned. Of course," he added gracefully, "Baptists aren't the only ones with that difficulty."

In person and on the phone, in countless interviews, I met women who were easy for me to identify with as they were struggling along the way with the God of Abraham, and Sarah—pondering what that God might be doing with their lives. Some of them felt they had the answer.

CHAPTER 14

Los Angeles

$\mathcal{M}$ARTHA

A KNOCK ON the front door of my Santa Fe home put me face to face with a thirteen-year-old boy dressed in armor. He bowed.

"Sir Joel here, ma'am. I'm here to protect the valley and be your knight."

He actually seemed to mean it.

I gave him some milk and cookies and vowed to call on him if I needed him. Yes, he certainly could continue to play on the property and use it for forts and battles and the joyous victories of youth. This, for him, was a political visit.

Who, I asked myself, was I, to turn down the protection of a knight?

A few weeks later I thought of Sir Joel again.

I had driven from home to Los Angeles and up from the

ocean, down the long, long, tree-lined drive in Mulholland Canyon. A farm was on the right side. The prefabricated buildings on the left looked as if they housed offices. A sentry house stood halfway down the mile-long entry. Russell, who went everywhere with me, rode in his car seat.

I tried to explain to the obviously dedicated guard at the sentry post that I was a reporter on assignment and that I wanted to talk to the woman who ran the place. He looked like Sir Joel from Cerro Gordo except that he was in his twenties, wore a suit and tie and had lost all sense of fun, play and perspective.

Some friends in Santa Fe had told me about this place called "Camelot" where a woman ran a religion and taught international spiritual politics. I thought perhaps there was a story in her work. I told the guard that I was writing a newspaper column on women and religion and saw a skeptical look on his face.

Isn't it odd to be surprised at a woman writer with a baby in the car when you yourself are standing in a sentry box at the door of a place with a sign that says, "Camelot"? I thought that it should be obvious to him that I was exactly who I said I was and not an agent of the Internal Revenue Service or a terrorist with a bomb in her BMW who might be willing to sacrifice a child for her cause. He didn't look convinced. I handed him a business card and wrote a note.

The next day I was summoned back to Camelot.

I left Russ with Mary Anne at the newspaper. She was a normal woman who happened to be the editor of a newspaper and who thought a baby in the newsroom was a bright spot in the day.

The woman who owned and ruled over Camelot turned out to be an unusual and newsworthy subject, a woman who controlled thousands and thousands of acres bordering Yellowstone Park, guns in bunkers, thousands of followers, a woman who described herself as Mother of the Universe. She was born in a small New Jersey town, to modest circumstance, a clarinet player in her high school band, she said. Now she lived in a castle on thirty-three acres of prime Southern California real estate.

We met in a large, drab upstairs reception room. She allowed as how she "had not yet turned her attention to" the room. One could understand, what with running the Universe and organizing bomb shelter preparation for the impending end of the world.

Over lunch of tofu burgers and sprouts, which she didn't touch, she described her third husband to me as an agent of Satan. I asked her if she had talked to any girlfriends about him; most would surely tell her that they had met at least one man like him in their lives.

She told me she talked only to the paid help and her

fourth husband, a wealthy orphan ten years younger than herself who believed her or at least purported to in public. Thousands of men and women believed her when she stood in front of them, with her videotape crew recording every moment, closed her eyes, put her ringed fingers to her head as if in a trance and said she was a channel for the voices of Gautama Buddha and Mary the Mother of Jesus and for her second and deceased husband, and a score of other men and women, some very well known, others obscure. Thousands gave her their money and their time and their children to raise.

She looked straight into my eyes and told me that she was the most highly evolved being on the planet. She had no more karma to work through. I noted a streak of competitiveness when she added, "Oh, I just knew you were going to wear pearls, too. Maybe I should change clothes for this interview."

Her eighteen-year-old son had the only reserved parking place on the grounds. Although she said she was a vegetarian and that everyone who lived in her feudal empire was vegetarian, her children were on their way to the local drive-in for some really good, meaty, red and juicy hamburgers.

She had never, never, never been without at least one man. I listened to her tell me that she knew she "lived a previous life in Egypt" as Nefertiti because when she was in her sandbox at age two she distinctly remembered being on a barge and getting confirmation from her mother that there were such things as special people and Egypt and previous lives.

There was the time she was Guinevere, which is why her place is named Camelot. And those times that she was one of several European queens as well as that time she was Martha as in Martha and Mary of Bethany, loved friends of Jesus of Nazareth.

It was that Mary which anointed the Lord with ointment, and wiped his feet with her hair, whose brother Lazarus was sick, says John.

Martha, Martha, Jesus says, *thou art careful and troubled about many things: But one thing is needful: and Mary hath chosen that good part, which shall not be taken away from her.*

I mentioned the text to her. Although each of the sisters had their distinct place and certain individuality, too much of my life had been troubled about many things so I could not imagine why anyone would want to be Martha.

"Mary Baker Eddy was my sister Mary," she said, as if that explained it. What I had read told me that the nineteenth century founder of The First Church of Christ, Scientist and the woman in front of me claiming to having been Martha represented two entirely separate schools of thought. Perhaps it was that competitive bent surfacing once more.

I felt a rush of compassion for this woman who actually had to live with herself day in and day out, never knowing from one minute to the next whether it would be Martha or Nefertiti, the Mother of Jesus or her own dead husband possessing her body. But I was a reporter here and not a comforter.

"How did you get all the good parts for girls through the ages?" I asked.

"Well," she said, "I wasn't always famous. Once I was just a bourgeois housewife in seventeenth century France."

She added, "But on my death bed the priest came to give me the last rites and when I looked into his eyes I knew that it was my twin flame through all eternity."

Her twin flame through all eternity was the second husband whose voice she still hears. It struck me as not particularly unusual to hear one of your husbands' voices if four of his children talk to you each and every day.

I felt she suffered from *folie grandeur* and that if she had sought psychiatric counseling she might have been described as having multiple personality disorder.

Ninety per cent of the people in the nation treated for

this condition are women. Psychologists and psychiatrists are discovering that parts of the self are so traumatized they split off from the main self and form separate identities and even separate wardrobes. I've asked myself if multiple personality disorder is similar to the condition of Mary Magdalene before Jesus cast seven devils out of her.

Was this woman an unhealed Mary Magdalene? Was she the repository for the tormenting passions of women who are denied proper channels for growth in the Church? An example of the dangers of pantheism in a democracy?

I began to experience a severe case of nausea. I was overwhelmed and could hardly breathe. I could scarcely keep myself in one piece as I drove down the Pacific Coast Highway to Santa Monica and barely made it into the house and the bathroom before I began a spasm of vomiting. Perhaps it was the tofu for lunch.

Followers of the Mother of the Universe would have said that my demons were being exorcised by exposure to her presence. My newspaper colleague, Mary Anne, who kept a hunting rifle next to the side of her bed, thought that Mother herself made me sick.

I talked Mary Anne into going with me to Camelot to see for herself.

"What keeps us from being like that, from being that woman?" I said on the drive back.

I stepped right into it.

"We don't take followers," she said, her eyes on the road straight ahead.

Women without followers told me stories that were affecting, sincere, so steeped in life experience that it was easy filling the column week after week. Besides, two ministers were running for President. Religion was not just on my mind, but everywhere.

CHAPTER 15

Albuquerque

CHURCH OF THE OPEN DOOR

ON ANY AUTUMN Monday night in the United States millions watch televised football in their living rooms. More millions go to church to watch televised preachers describe the end of the world.

At the Church of the Open Door in Albuquerque I sat with several hundred others watching one of those preachers. By satellite, larger than life, stem-winding his way through biblical interpretations, ten feet tall, in a three-piece suit, he quoted from the Book of Revelation with a delivery in the line of William Jennings Bryan.

The television screen was in front of the altar. Barely visible behind the screen was the cross. On the left-hand wall were the words, "WORKING TOGETHER TELLING THE WORLD." On the right, "JESUS CHRIST, THE SAME YES-TERDAY, TODAY AND FOREVER" and an American flag. On the screen, the church set looked like the West Wing of the White House. The windows opened on to something resembling the White House Rose Garden. The church that I sat in looked as spare as a U.S. Army chapel in a foreign outpost.

I felt as if I were a foreign correspondent taking notes as a warm-up preacher pointed out to us, in audiences around the nation, that "just because you are seeing me on the screen doesn't mean that Jesus isn't here."

He told us to make friends with our money because money is power. The lights dimmed on the screen and a collection was taken. I felt a long way from a group of fishermen and carpenters and tent makers healing the sick and raising the dead; from women who ministered to a young, single man identified as the Christ.

The main preacher appeared in front of the Rose Garden mock-up. His politics were his theology. "Israel is not an armed camp, it is an arsenal," he said as a plane, from the sound track on the screen or from Kirtland Air Force Base some miles away, broke the sound barrier.

The preacher told us in gory detail that the Bible says Israel is going to destroy China; that World War III is not Armageddon; and that in forty-five minutes Jesus is going to take care of it all with a sword. The good guys win.

He said that all the enemies of America are to be destroyed by fulfillment of biblical prophecy and that there is nothing that we in the viewing audience have to do about it. It is preordained. However, a toll-free number flashed on the screen for more information. Nothing was left to the imagination, nothing to free inquiry.

Later, driving up the highway to Santa Fe, past the Indian pueblos, over La Bajada hill, I turned on the radio to a call-in show.

"Reverend," said the woman caller, "I've been having a problem with a verse in 2nd Corinthians and I wonder if you could explain it for me?"

The radio preacher went on talking about Jesus and what he did and about what Paul meant when he wrote that letter to the Corinthians. He rearranged the words of the letter and repeated them with no explanation. The woman said, "Oh thank you, I've really been struggling with that." As he prepared to move on, she blurted out, "Oh, and by the way could you say a prayer for my son? He's really a good boy."

I was alone in my car. The woman was alone in her room some place in another state, alone with her pride and her love for her son who, I envisioned, had probably come home yesterday with needle marks in his arm, or something in a brown paper bag that was not his left-over lunch. Perhaps he was being pressured to join a gang. All this woman could do was to call a remote authority figure and ask him to pray for her son. The man said, "Sure," and hung up. The woman was left alone in her room hoping for help. I ached for that woman, for me, for all women who weren't getting from their pastors exactly what they needed.

It took some time after arriving at home, after I had lit a fire, checked the children in their beds, and made a cup of tea before I could feel any warmth at all.

The gap between practice and preaching is greater than my soul can bear. Where were *the pastors according to our hearts,* not their hearts but ours, the widows and the orphans?

> *Which is the way where light dwells,*
> *And which is the place of darkness,*
> *That you may take it to its border,*
> *And that you may perceive the paths*
> *to its home?*
>
> *You know, for you were born then,*
> *And the number of your days is great!*
>
> *Have you been to the storehouses of snow,*
> *Or do you see the storehouses of hail,*
> *Which I have reserved against the*
> *time of distress,*

Against the day of war and battle?
Which is the way to where light is
distributed?
Where does the east wind spread itself
over the earth?

PART FOUR

*I*n that day, saith the Lord, will I assemble
her that halteth, and I will gather her that is
driven out, and her that I have afflicted,

And thou, O tower of the flock, the strong
hold of the daughter of Zion, unto thee it shall
come, even the first dominion; the kingdom shall
come to the daughter of Jerusalem.

MICAH 4: 6, 8

CHAPTER 16

Santa Fe

REDEEMING HOLINESS

I COULDN'T SAY, like Paul, that in one moment on a certain road in a certain place I was converted. Delivered. Yes. Many times. Spared. Yes. Blessed. That too. Any one of the biblical encounters I did have might have been enough for some. I had used the Bible, thought of it as a friend that was there when needed. Paul was so sure, so definite, he never, we think, like Lot's wife—like me— looked back.

But a moment did come that was unlike other moments. I can't say what hour it was by the clock but the moment was clear. It came not on a road but in a newsroom in Santa Fe. I was working on a story about Paul's influence on contemporary politics. Some women had no problem with Paul. Some women were troubled by him and saw him as the ultimate sexist. Others took his words reported in Ephesians, *Wives, submit yourselves unto your own husbands, as unto the Lord,* as a mandate to vote the way their husbands told them to.

Hundreds of women had complained to me about Paul, hundreds more had told me they were conflicted. They believed but they were having a hard time dealing with *wives, submit yourselves unto your own husbands.* In an attempt to be biblically correct, many of these women had voted for not their own but their husband's choice for President. My job, I thought, was to put Paul into perspective for them so they might vote their own prayerful conscience.

My perspective on Paul was fairly liberal. He was after all just a man. And, unmarried, I voted, for better or worse, based on my own knowledge and opinions. Neither his humanity nor my opinions gave me any particular insight into Paul or why, dead two thousand years, still had a say, as he had recently, in electing American Presidents.

I had a list to call, people to interview on the topic. Down at the bottom of the list was a name given to me by a long-time friend, which is how a journalist often develops an interview list and one of the reasons there are not as many innovations in journalism as there might be.

One call led to another. "I heard this guy say something in a church I was visiting about ten years ago," she said. "What he said stuck with me. Try him."

She had read the deep messages of the Bible the twenty years I had known her. She pondered them, lived them. What swayed me was that something said ten years ago "stuck" with her.

I was standing at my desk, an editor behind me was shouting at a photographer about a police call, two dozen other people were working at their computers or on the phone, some minions were carrying stacks of paper from desk to desk, the fluorescent lights were giving off their stingy hum, the air was stale from a day of work with no open windows. I explained that I was a journalist writing about Paul, husbands, wives, and the vote.

He said that many women had told him they were conflicted about Paul.

"So many women have a deep, deep hurt about the way the Bible is interpreted," he said.

And then he asked me if I had a Bible handy.

I opened my purse.

"When Paul was reminiscing on spiritual creation in Ephesians 5," he began and I caught my breath and sat down.

This was news.

It might not seem like anything at all to one who has never lost sleep over Paul.

Paul reminiscing?

Paul exhorting. That I had heard. Saul, Paul *breathing out threatenings and slaughter*. That I had also heard. Paul preaching. But reminiscing? Not Paul. I had never thought of him as contemplative, reflective. Historical, important, zealous, but not deep, not reflective, not reminiscing.

I had lived life on a rather wide scale and yet, in this moment, God, for me, was definitely in the details.

This voice on the other end of the phone lifted a veil from the text. I looked beyond the veil into the text. I listened to Paul writing and talking to his friends in Ephesus. I saw Paul separating the male and female of God's creating from Adam and Eve, reblending it again, as he ached that men and women did not understand the equality of all relationships. I heard him as he tried to give information that could change forever the way his listeners thought about themselves, about God, about spiritual Creation.

Wives, submit yourselves to your own husbands, as unto the Lord.

Not as unto your husband. But as to the Lord.

For the husband is the head of the wife, even as Christ is the head of the church; and he is the saviour of the body.

The relationship of the wife to the husband is as the relationship of Christ to the body of the church.

Husbands, love your wives, even as Christ also loved the church, and gave himself for it;

How did Christ love the Church?

He washed the feet of the Church when he washed the feet of the disciples. And, there is the cross and the Resurrection.

For this cause shall a man leave his father and mother, and shall be joined unto his wife, and they two shall be one flesh. This is a great mystery: but I speak concerning Christ and the church. Nevertheless let every one of you in particular so love his wife even as himself; and the wife see that she reverence her husband.

By his own definition literalness didn't begin to explain what Paul was talking about. But John, who reports that Jesus' mother urged her son's ministry to begin at a wedding, must have been addressing the issue of translating the literal into the spiritual. Leaving biological parenthood for a relationship symbolized by water—washing the feet, changing water into wine—was diving to depths I hadn't begun to comprehend.

I knew for sure—then in that newsroom—what I had always known somewhere in the depth of my heart. Reading isn't always reading. It's possible to read and read and study and study and come up with the same old, tired literalness that perhaps drives some Western women to think of a journey to Tibet as the sure road of escape from the Bible.

Every sentence, every word of Paul's reminiscences on spiritual Creation opened up reflections on the possibilities of unique individuality, on service to and being serviced by the Creation described in Genesis 1, where verse twenty-seven says, *male and female created he them.*

With one hand on the telephone receiver and the other on the Bible, I began to fantasize about what would happen to the United States if all Christian men washed their wives' feet while saying, "Who do you think we should vote for this time? Would you like to see a President who made sure no child went to bed hungry?"

My fantasy stopped short when the voice on the other end of the line started talking about Mary telling Jesus that it was time to turn the water into wine and I saw the scene. "Stop," I said. "I can't go any further now."

It is possible to believe that a man or a woman was changed, that something happened to him or her. But the process is individual, perhaps suggestive, and not easily translated. That is, I think, one reason Paul felt impelled to repeat his conversion. He refers to it in letters to the Galatians, the Ephesians, Corinthians, to Timothy.

Conversion is inward, it seems Paul is saying, it is not observance of law, not repetition of liturgy. Reminding oneself of one's history keeps it from getting lost in abstraction.

I am the Lord that brought thee out of Ur of the Chaldees, to give thee this land to inherit it, God reminds Abram.

And he reminds Moses—who then repeats to the people—*I am the Lord thy God, which have brought thee out of the land of Egypt, out of the house of bondage.*

Remember who you were, where you are and how you got here.

Paul tells his personal story and to this day the personal story is the way to remember where one has been and how much further one must go.

Fragmentary, whole, imperfect, nearly perfect, self-centered, selfless, believable, unbelievable, revised, expunged, in the repetition, in the narrative, in the listening is the seed of identity.

This newsroom plunge into the spirit of the Bible texts filled me with a sadness, a solemnity occasioned by the gap between my everyday life and the momentary glimpse I caught of the seamlessness of the Book. I wanted nothing more than to search the Scriptures—to learn what I didn't know.

I sold my property, the cars, the furniture, gave my children their financial inheritance and moved to a small cottage outside Santa Fe where I began to read the Bible with yet again different eyes. I began to read the Bible as journalistic dispatches from the spiritual front. I checked sources, looked at stories told in differing accounts, followed themes. I dissected, relented, allowed new ideas and images into my interpretations and reflections. I began to feel as if I were in Israel.

Jerusalem

SHEKINAH

WITHIN MONTHS, THROUGH the grace of an assignment, I went to Israel. I went to photograph a book cover, spent a glorious week in Tel Aviv, and then took a month exploring Jerusalem and Bethlehem, walking the shores of the Galilee and interviewing women about the Bible as a narrative of spiritual power through and for women. Pnina Peli was one of them.

Pnina Peli is a leading figure of Orthodox theology in Israel. We had much to talk about. During the time that I was writing about women and religion in the United States, Pnina was doing a weekly radio show in Israel and we compared notes.

The sun streamed in the window of her apartment through lace curtains, bathing the plants on the window sill in light so clear that all the colors can be seen in it as in the rainbow. The walls were weighted with shelves of books in Hebrew and English.

Pnina told me that she was born Betty in Brooklyn and at seventeen married the rabbi, and became an Israeli citizen when she moved with her husband to Jerusalem. I told her about my marriage. We talked about our religious concerns.

We discussed the question of the Shekinah in today's world. Shekinah, the in-dwelling female Principle of God to some, is the "glory" to others.

And it came to pass, as Aaron spake unto the whole congregation of the children of Israel, that they looked toward the wilderness, and, behold, the glory of the Lord appeared in the cloud.

"Defining the undefined and only partially recalled identity of the Shekinah is the main task of Judaism," Pnina said as she poured the tea. As two grandmothers in their forties might, we had reached a certain plateau of life and concern.

"Abraham may have received the promise but Sarai is the source of the Shekinah. Abraham was inferior to Sarah in the area of prophecy," Pnina said quoting the Talmud. "She kept a candle lit from Friday evening to Saturday evening which did not go out."

The Hebrew word for light, fire, is also a word for woman and Shekinah. And the essence of renaming is from Sarah actualized—the name Israel comes from Sarah. Jacob is a follower of Sarah. Sarah, not Eve, is the mother of Us All. "There is no question about it," she said.

Abigail, Huldah, and the other women prophets were real women involved in keeping the peace and rousing thought to another, higher level. It did not seem odd to me when Pnina added, "The involvement of real women is central to peace in Israel and the reception of the Messiah. Our job is to keep on redeeming Holiness. Our job is to keep saying, in every way possible, that mankind is not instinctive but spiritual. I think Rachel and Leah are crying because the Shekinah is not fulfilled in this world."

I was on home ground. Not the only one who thinks of biblical women as real, as specific illustrative examples of the female psyche. Nor the only one who thinks that the lives of biblical women intersect with personal life here and now. Any denominational histories and styles of worship evaporated before our common interest, our American high school experience as women thirsting for the spiritual.

"I went with my daughter to the Western Wall just before her marriage last year," Pnina said. "And I could see Shekinah weeping on the other side of the Wall. On one hand is the dualistic thinking that says there are two worlds, the material and the spiritual. On the other, those who kill Jews for witnessing for over five thousand years to the idea of One God. Caught between concepts of time, space and people, Israel is a house divided against itself.

"You know," she added, "the book of Esther is one of two books in the Bible that doesn't mention God. Perhaps the Shekinah went into exile then."

With the world in the state it is we agree there is no time to play tennis while Rome burns.

There was, however, time for lunch. Pnina and I agreed to meet again and some days later we sat across from each other at a small Italian restaurant just outside the center of Jerusalem. Pnina ordered a carafe of wine to go with the soup and salad, and when that was gone, I ordered some more and that's about the time we came up with the idea of visiting America's leading woman theologian, a title bestowed upon her by the press.

Pnina had heard that this woman was at Tantur, a study center outside town. She had not called Pnina, an oversight, we agreed, but as we were sure, at that moment, who we were and what we were doing, we decided to get in Pnina's car and just pop over to say hello.

In the car we talked about the future of our children in the next millennium, the emergence of the Motherhood of God as a given in human consciousness, about the history of the landscape out the windows. In the parking lot, standing by the car, Pnina suddenly looked down at her outfit and up at me and said, "Look at me in slacks and a sweater. I should have dressed."

"Hey, Betty, forget it," I said. "We can't be on the theological cutting edge wondering whether we should have dressed for the occasion."

Pretensions shattered, we were laughing so hard I was bent over holding my sides and Pnina had to rest on the side of the car to catch her breath.

The woman was ill with flu. But, hearing from the receptionist that she had visitors, she shuffled down the hall in her bathrobe, with a box of tissues in her hand. Her husband stood over her, protecting her as best he could from the Orthodox Jew in the slacks and the Protestant in jeans.

He said that their trip to Israel was to do some archeological digging. They were looking into the possibility of early Palestinian settlements with an eye to establishing Palestinian claims to Israel.

"What? He said what?" Pnina said on the way back to the car.

Theology, we agreed, on the silent ride back to Jerusalem, was not in pots and shards. Nor was God.

CHAPTER 18

Jerusalem/Megiddo

THE PILGRIM

IT WAS NEARLY noon. In the high vaulted international transit lounge at Charles De Gaulle airport, fifty born-again, evangelical, Pentecostal Christians formed a circle. They were wearing powder-blue windbreakers. Cameras hung around the necks of several of the men.

"Lord Jesus," said George, leader of this tour to the Holy Land, "we know that you are the Prince of Paris and that no terrorist bombs can harm us." Not one of them wanted to be in Paris, or for that matter on this earth. They were persuaded that war was biblically prophecied, that Jesus was returning to earth, and that both war and the bodily return of the Lord couldn't happen soon enough. George took my hand and there we were, fifty-one American Christians praying out loud in a circle while the handful of Europeans in the lounge glanced our way, bemused. The prayer ended. The light was clear and bright in our small, roped-off area of the hall.

As a reporter, I am tracking the story that the leaders of this group of fundamentalists who believe in a coming Apocalypse were deeply involved with the Defense Department and the White House. But as a human, I am not convinced that I can sleep in a room with anyone who wants the world to blow up so Jesus can come again to earth.

The plane, delayed on take-off in Washington, had missed the scheduled connection to Tel Aviv. George scurried around making arrangements for a new flight, an airport hotel, and a bus to take us on an hour-long tour of the City of Light.

Finally on the bus, we discovered that the driver, an Algerian, spoke no English. I was the only one on the tour with even a nodding acquaintance of French. The driver looked at me in disbelief when I told him the people were not getting out of the bus but planned to view the Eiffel Tower and all the other wonderful sights of Paris from behind double-thick glass.

Then the other women on the bus watched, in what they described to me later as astonishment, as I got into a taxi at the nearest stand and set off to they knew not where. How, they wondered, could a woman alone in a foreign country know where she was going? I could not believe we all read the same Bible. The story of Ruth and Naomi flickered through my mind as I watched the city glide by on my way to meet my friend Elizabeth. The last time we had been together was in a refugee camp on the Cambodian border.

The taxi pulled up in front of a large black gate. I rang the buzzer.

When Elizabeth heard about my impending tour, she said that it sounded stark. We dressed for dinner and were joined by other guests.

Someone mentioned Jonestown.

"That's not funny," I said.

"But this time," he said, "they are going to take everyone with them. Not just the believers."

It was early when I arrived at Charles De Gaulle. I had an espresso, read the *Herald Tribune,* picked at a croissant as if I were condemned and this my last meal.

The group arrived. I walked up trying to look cheery and rested although I was not. Two women told me that they had prayed for me and that George had said a special prayer on the bus coming over from the airport hotel that I would be delivered safely back to the group. It is obvious to them that God answered George's prayers because there I was.

On my Walkman, Handel and his *Solomon* soothed and encouraged me through the flight to Israel.

"We want to go straight to the Mount of Olives. We are tired but we want to go right away and then we will come back and check in the hotel," George said. We boarded the waiting tour bus outside the Tel Aviv airport.

People cheered and we set off around the winding road down the hill and up again until we reached the Mount of Olives with the walls of the Old City of Jerusalem eight hundred meters away, gleaming in the late afternoon sun. George intoned, "Here, here, on this very spot, Our Lord will set foot on the earth any day now. It could be right now while we are in the Holy Land on this tour.

"The earth will cleave in two and a river will run down there and you will all rule with Jesus in Jerusalem for a thousand years." Applause rang out, for both the performance and the message.

Dinner is full of conversation about how many Christians of this particular variety are in the White House.

In the morning as the bus rolled down the highway past the Dead Sea I heard George's wife, Virginia, talking about the determination of Deborah in battle and of Jael as she drove a stake through Sisera's head.

Virginia chose her heroines with care. Of the seven women prophets of Israel, Deborah is the one with military experience, and with Esther, one who has no hesitation concerning the death of enemies to her nation. Deborah sat under a palm tree and judged Israel, went into battle with men who wouldn't go without her. Under her leadership the enemy fled. And in an elegant display of mimetic desire, another woman, Jael, invited the ieader of Israel's enemies into her tent and after lulling him to sleep with some milk, drove a stake through his head with the hammer she kept by her bed.

At Masada, I first talked to George about his vision. George stood alone with his back to the mountain fortress.

"I'm not familiar with your particular views," I said, "and I wonder if you can explain to me what you see and how you got into this line of work."

"There," George said, sweeping his hand down the barren hills to the Sea of Salt, "is God's destruction of sin. This is Sodom and Gomorrah."

"How did you come to lead tours to Israel?" I asked glancing to my right and seeing only barrenness.

A jet engine split the air. George looked up and said, "That's a Kaffir." I asked him how he knew the sound of one engine from another. He was the former chief executive officer of one of the United States' leading jet aircraft manufacturers, he said, and that answered most of my questions.

"Virginia was a secretary at the company," he said, looking across the concrete to the soft drink stand where his wife sat with three other women. "And she brought me to the Lord."

Virginia, Bible open, gesticulating as she turned, was proselytizing a woman who said that she was a member of the Church of Jesus Christ of Latter Day Saints. I sensed a stalemate.

At lunch, at the base of Masada, several people at the table were startled and afraid of the sounds of jets in the air. George told them what a hot bed of military activity we were in, with democracy being under such severe threats from the outside, but that the Air Force of Israel would keep us safe.

I ask George how it is possible to want the world to end so Jesus can come back and yet be afraid that it might all end before lunch.

Where my traveling companions had been living, while the scientific concept of matter exploded, rearranged itself, I am not sure. To say, as some observers do, that they had been in small towns, outside the mainstream, in captivity to old theology, is a sociological oversimplification.

The men and women on this trip, even the children, were very much in touch with social trends and had more than a nodding acquaintance with politics. At dinner that night a general in the Israeli military would explain the beleaguered position of his tiny country and the need of support from the likes of George for the People of God. No, these pilgrims were not uninformed people. One of the men was a scientist at the Livermore Lab in California working on military secrets. I've lived close enough to Los Alamos to know that in the world of weapons, flights from Albuquerque to San Francisco are equivalent to the New York-to-Washington shuttles.

It is just that my reading of the Bible—the one that says God is love, the kingdom of heaven is at hand and within—was apparently not the same as theirs. The particular brand of Pentecostal belief that dominated this group took the concrete present and abstracted it into a future salvation linked to the second appearing of a personal Jesus.

The next day as we all stood in a large stone room in the old city of Jerusalem, George hopped onto the stage and announced that this was the Upper Room where the followers of Jesus met after the crucifixion and where, the Book of Acts says, *On the day of the Harvest Festival, they were all meeting together, when suddenly there came from the sky a sound like a violent blast of wind, and it filled the whole house where they were sitting. And they saw tongues like flames separating and seething one on each of them, and they were all filled with the Holy Spirit and began to say in foreign languages whatever the Spirit prompted them to utter.*

*   *   *

One of the women came up to me, put her arm around my waist and said with a smile, "Sugar, we are all praying for you to receive the Holy Spirit."

I leaned over and whispered back, "How do you know that I don't have it?"

Outside, waiting for the group to pile back in the buses, one of the Israeli guides, Joe, whispered to me, "The place where we stand couldn't possibly be the Upper Room. It wasn't built until about 1100 A.D." I asked how he got into this line of work and how he knew so much about Christianity. "I marched to Selma with Martin Luther King," he said, "and was in jail with a lot of priests and ministers. The only book prisoners were allowed to read was the Bible." I asked him how he could stand doing these tours.

"Here's how," he said. "I tell myself that the Christians on my bus last week were blasphemers. The Christians on my bus next week will be heretics. The ones on the bus this week are the true Christians."

The next morning no one would sit next to me on the bus.

There is no place on earth more beautiful than southern Lebanon in early March. A light rain was falling and it was early evening. Orchards spread out framed against the mountains. The slight green of the buds on the fruit trees was light against the purple-tinged mist of the rain and the air. The flowers of the trees looked like puffs of white snow at the tips of one's fingers. A dog barked somewhere up a tree-lined, stone street, a motorcycle could be heard in the distance.

Is it not a very little while, and Lebanon shall be turned into a fruitful field, and the fruitful field shall be esteemed as a forest? The meek shall also increase their joy in the Lord.

In Isaiah's prophecy I almost forgot that we were very, very close to Tyre and Sidon and Syria.

We spent a quiet night in the hills of Lebanon and after breakfast, on the bus rolling back down the road, I could hear George saying, "We are going to the most exciting spot on earth," at the same time that I was exclaiming out loud about the view where we were.

George's most exciting spot on earth was Megiddo, the Valley of Armageddon, and he really got worked up about it as the bus wound down the road from the mountains and pulled up at a place where Solomon built a gate like the one at the Temple in Jerusalem.

At the top of the hill Joe paused and said, "Over there

Elijah healed the widow woman, on the other side of the hill is where Jesus healed a widow woman. What happens over here in the Old Testament happens over there in the New." I wondered if the full implication of Joe's message settled into the minds connected with these smiling, sincere faces.

"Below us is where Deborah led the armies of Israel in her successful battle. You will notice that there is only one road through this valley and should there be any future invaders, say from the north . . . ," said Joe. He played on the geography and the tourists' fears by alluding to biblical verses dear to the Apocalyptic Mind, which refer to kings and armies from the north, and, pausing for effect, said, "Well then, ladies and gentlemen, Welcome to Armageddon."

Now it was George's turn. He waited for a moment and then, standing on a rock outcropping, he pointed to a hole in a large cumulus cloud above saying, in a perfect fifteen-second sound bite, "There, right through there, Jesus will come on a white horse and freeze frame time."

The Revelation of John puts it this way: *And I saw heaven opened, and behold a white horse; and he that sat upon him was called Faithful and True, and in righteousness he doth judge and make war.*

The group loved the sight of George, wind blowing in

his hair, Bible open in one hand and the other hand raised, finger pointing to the sky where Jesus would be any minute.

"Isn't this exciting," said one of the men, taking the hand of the woman nearest him. "Just think. Any day now this valley will be full of blood." Several members of the group cheered.

The buses stopped at Caesarea, which consists of a few ruins, some rocks, sand and shore. It is the place where Jesus asked the most profound question the ages have recorded, *Whom say ye that I am?*

It was at Caesarea that Jesus said to Peter, *Upon this rock I will build my church.*

Philip was transported there directly from his meeting by the water with the eunuch treasurer of Queen Candace of Ethiopia.

Peter visited Cornelius in Caesarea and recounted to him the meaning of Deuteronomy 10, *regardeth not persons, nor talketh reward: He doth execute the judgment of the fatherless and widow, and loveth the stranger, in giving him food and raiment.*

This statement from the Torah traces itself through Peter's vision to the book of James where to *visit the fatherless and the widows in their affliction* is described as *pure and undefiled religion.* Philip and his four prophetess daughters lived at Caesarea; Paul was there more than once; King Agrippa and Queen Bernice came to visit; and all in all to visit Caesarea is to live in much of the Book of Acts.

The early church is present amid the rocks and the stones and the sand and the water.

George talked about sixty thousand dollars he needed for a new building and some land, and before you could say Jack Robinson, George had his sixty thousand dollars in cash and checks.

When all the money had been counted, George took the microphone. "With this sixty thousand dollars you've just dealt Satan a death blow."

He looked up and saw the expression on my face; I was clearly dumbstruck by his trivialization of evil in the world.

"You think so too, don't you, don't you," he shouted as he came toward me, cheeks red, fire in his eyes, shoving the microphone in my face.

Dear Father-Mother God, I said to myself. Please put words in my mouth.

"It couldn't hurt," I heard myself say.

Three women, each for her own purposes, left the tour a day early to head back to Jerusalem. George had our bags dropped on the side of the street across from the public bus terminal. Dragging and hauling her suitcases across a dirt strip between the sidewalk and the street, one woman fell. A local citizen stopped to see if he could help, but the woman on the ground snapped at him, "No." An Arab shopkeeper came over from his store and offered her a chair.

Another citizen stopped and said, "You can't hurt yourself, this is holy ground."

But the woman wanted none of their help or support. The other woman and I helped her pull herself up and she asked if we could form a circle and close our eyes and say a prayer.

I do my praying silently and in private but I like to think of myself as a good sport, so I stood there while she said, "We know, Dear Jesus, that nothing can keep us from getting on the bus and getting to Jerusalem."

I smiled and waved and thanked the kind men who practiced their religion and were rebuffed.

Enough was enough. I put them with their suitcases in line and went to buy tickets for the next bus. When we arrived at the Central Bus Terminal in Jerusalem in blinding and bitter snow, and they looked terrified and lost, I lent one woman my sweater, and put them under a shelter until I could find a cab.

Scouting around, I hassled a driver to cancel another call and agree to drop me at the King David Hotel and take the other two women to the Armenian Quarter of the Old City where they had arranged to stay in a Christian hotel.

I was the fairy godmother who arrived with a coach and horses, and a new gown for the ball. So they thought. I had, by their lights, done something out of the ordinary and really wonderful by not leaving them freezing and helpless in the snow. They went on and on about how kind I was. They were used to being left and being helpless. I had found the line of demarcation on our respective approaches to God.

The God they worshipped was a man they feared, who they thought had left them and who they hoped was coming back some day to get them, a day in which there would be no clothing crisis, no questioning what to wear, no suitcases heavier than could be carried over the shoulder.

The God that I worship is a *very present help in trouble* for women getting taxis in the snow of Jerusalem at the very moment they need them.

I came home and painted the words of God to Moses on the entry hall floor of my house and painted over the fireplace a rainbow.

I do set my bow in the cloud, and it shall be for a token of a covenant between me and the earth.

That the bow shall be seen in the cloud:

And the bow shall be in the cloud; and I will look upon it, that I may remember the everlasting covenant between God and every living creature of all flesh that is upon the earth.

———

Russ and Hannah thought it was for them, which it was.

Over the bookshelves I painted, in rainbow colors, the names of each of the seven women prophets of Israel: Sarah, Miriam, Deborah, Hannah, Abigail, Huldah, Esther. Those names were for me.

CHAPTER 19

Tesuque, New Mexico

*S*EA OF GLASS

WHEN I LIVED in the desert on the edge of the Mexican border, I often took my children on horseback up into the mountains for all-day rides. My daughter would ride on the horse behind me while I held the reins, and my son, not yet walking, would sit in front of me in my saddle. At four o'clock we tied our horses up to the porch of the ranch house where I rented the horses, the only house for twenty miles. We sat on the big leather rockers on the porch watching the sun begin its descent over the mountains as we waited for the owner to call us in to supper.

Verna, the owner's wife, made bread. Next to my grandmother's, it was the best bread I ever tasted. I had tried unsuccessfully for several years to make regular white bread, the kind with the thick crust, the kind that butter melts into. Verna told me how to master the art. Put in a bowl:

Four tablespoons of salad oil.

Four tablespoons of sugar.

Two tablespoons of salt.

About five cups of warm water poured over the top so that the sugar would dissolve.

Two packages of dry yeast until it bubbles and then enough flour mixed in to make a kneadable bunch.

Knead, set aside for about twenty minutes.

Punch down.

Divide into two or three loaves.

Put in cake baking pan with the sides touching each other.

Let sit another twenty minutes.

Bake at 375° for forty-five minutes.

No eggs, no milk. No mystery. Simple perfection.

Yet achieving perfection took me flour on the ceiling and the floor. Flour in my nails, loaves thrown away, sacks and sacks of flour before kneading became second nature and baking bread became a part of my daily life, evidence of simple sustenance, something I could offer people who were my guests.

At some point I got the knack, the resistant piece of dough became something my hands could handle, my fingers could feel, my outstretched arms could know, had become the loaf of bread that fire and heat would present to our eager mouths and stomachs.

My relationship to the Bible was not unlike my relationship to bread. It seemed easy when I first followed a recipe. Then I went through a long period when I tried and tried to make it my own, tried to get a handle on a huge lump of sticky stuff that bore no seeming relationship to what it would become. Everything was all over the place. A mess.

And one day the whole thing came together.

I could almost hear Mary say to Luke, "I was walking from my bedroom to the kitchen to get something to eat and I heard a voice. Someone had come in when I was reading. He greeted me, and then he said, *thou art highly favoured, the Lord is with thee: blessed art thou among women.*

When she saw him, she *was troubled at his saying, and cast in her mind what manner of salutation this should be.*

Naturally she wondered, and he said *with God nothing shall be impossible.*

That story, now abstracted and decorated, is called the Visitation in art and church lore. That extrapolation makes it rather difficult to identify the story for what it actually is: the tale of a young Jewish woman who, after the encounter, went to visit her cousin Elizabeth. What did the two women talk about in those pregnant months?

I found myself in the same circumstance and with the same God as Sarah, as Hagar, as Miriam, Deborah, Rachel and Leah, Ruth, Naomi, Hannah and Mary Magdalene, Elizabeth and Mary in the history of the women of Israel.

What I see about myself from this perspective is a woman on a journey from Eve to Mary of Magdala, struggling with temptations and guilt in the garden of human life.

Admitting mistakes and moving along again through the spiritual, emotional, physical peaks and valleys described in the Bible, I look out from the stars to the woman ahead of me, the woman described in the Book of Revelation *with the moon under her feet and a crown of twelve stars upon her head*.

Luke was a reporter who interviewed eyewitnesses and ministers to the events, the life of Jesus of Nazareth. He says, in the gospel that he addresses to *Theophilus* (friend of God), that he undertook the writing of his report in order to bring to remembrance what he knew, what many of his time knew.

Those who spend lifetimes studying such things as the possible dates the gospels were written disagree by several decades as to when Luke wrote his report. But by some estimations, if Jesus' mother, or Mary Magdalene, lived into their seventies, they may have talked to Luke. It would explain why he reports that an angel appeared, not as Matthew writes, to Joseph, but to Mary, why he records what Mary kept in her heart.

Who were these eyewitnesses he talked to? What did they tell him? Who were the ministers? Luke says, *And Simon's wife's mother was taken with a great fever; and they besought him for her. And he stood over her, and rebuked the fever; and it left her: and immediately she arose and ministered unto them.*

And certain women, which had been healed of evil spirits and infirmities, Mary called Magdalene, out of whom went seven devils, and Joanna, the wife of Chuza, Herod's servant, and Susanna, and many others, which ministered to him of their substance.

Why did these women leave homes and husbands to minister to Jesus? Where did they think they were going?

While I am seen traveling in different clothes, in different countries, in different times with different people, going first one way and then another, missing the turn by miles, light years or by only a fraction of a second, on the mark from time to time, God sees me, says the Bible, in white, radiant, pure, beyond virginal, including male and female as my being, open, yielding, welcoming, and at one with the Lamb.

In the meantime I go from Eve to Sarai, following her nomadic and ambitious and clever husband through the desert from tent to tent. Three men come to visit them, her husband entertains them and she knows that she will conceive when it is impossible, that God will come to her flesh, that as Sarah her seed shall live forever.

I follow Sarah to Miriam and I walk through the wilderness and through the ebbing and flowing of the Red Sea of human thoughts, through fear and desire to turn back like Lot's wife.

I look again and see myself urging my children and myself on to an extremely uncertain future all the while singing with Miriam.

Miriam's song melts into Hannah's song.

There is none holy as the Lord: for there is none beside thee: neither is there any rock like our God. Talk no more so exceedingly proudly; let not arrogancy come out of your mouth: for the Lord is a God of knowledge, and by him actions are weighed.

The Lord maketh poor, and maketh rich: he bringeth low, and lifteth up.

And Hannah's song weaves into Mary's.

He hath put down the mighty from their seats, and exalted them of low degree. He hath filled the hungry with good things; and the rich he hath sent empty away.

Finding moral leadership lacking among the males of my nation I look to find a Deborah leading nations, challenging indecision and lack of moral courage in the midst of war. Deborah did not moan and groan about the state of the army and politics. She judged.

I struggle for the grace, foresight and the spiritual and political wisdom of Abigail and wait to greet the King, David, the poet, the mad dancer, the impassioned inclusionary representative of the God of Israel, and wait, too, as the warrior in me yields to the diplomat.

I ponder on Huldah sitting by the temple answering questions on matters concerning the law and the future. Along with many others I am Esther in exile.

I am the King's daughter, all glorious within, I am waiting for the eagles to come to me and nourish me. I am crying in the streets for my beloved.

I am a part of all the Miriams and Marys, Mary of Magdala, the other Mary, the unnamed woman. Seen and not seen, known and not known, in and out of the narrative of the times and yet I am here, now, trying to look at my life through the lives of the women in the Bible and through the mist, in the midst of my own particular circumstance.

I have yet to do more than glimpse the bottom of the laver that the women who went with Miriam through the Red Sea hammered into being from their mirrors, yet to lose myself in a sea of glass.

I have yet to live forever in the Holy City.

With God nothing shall be impossible, Gabriel told Mary.

Not easy, but not impossible.

$\mathcal{S}$ O U R C E S

Biblical selections are from the King James Version of the Bible or from the Tanakh, *published by the Jewish Publication Society.*

P R O L O G U E :

Now when Jesus . . . Mark 16:9
And their words . . . Luke 24:11
He makes me lie down . . . Psalm 23, *Tanakh,* The Holy Scriptures, Jewish Publication Society
Put off thy shoes . . . Exodus 3:5

C H A P T E R   T W O :

Before I formed thee . . . Jeremiah 1:5

C H A P T E R   T H R E E :

Enlarge the place of thy tent . . . Isaiah 54:2
For the mountains shall depart . . . Isaiah 54:10
The Lord appeared . . . Genesis 18:1
Ho, everyone that thirsteth . . . Isaiah 55:1

For my thoughts . . . Isaiah 55:8
For ye shall go out with joy . . . Isaiah 55:12
As one whom his mother . . . Isaiah 66:13
And the Lord God formed . . . Genesis 2:7
And the Lord God commanded . . . Genesis 2:16
God doth know . . . Genesis 3:5–7
And I saw a new heaven . . . Revelation 21:1–5
Ho, everyone that thirsteth . . . Isaiah 55:1
And the Spirit and the bride . . . Revelation 22:17

C H A P T E R   F O U R :

For the mountains shall . . . Isaiah 54:10
For ye shall go out with joy . . . Isaiah 55:12

C H A P T E R   F I V E :

And they came . . . Exodus 35:21
The laver of brass . . . Exodus 38:8
And I heard a great voice . . . Revelation 21:3
Then a cloud covered the tent . . . Exodus 40:34

C H A P T E R   S I X :

A woman of the city . . . Luke 7:37
Her sins, which are many . . . Luke 7:47
Of a truth I perceive . . . Acts 10:34

C H A P T E R   S E V E N :

For the mountains shall . . . Isaiah 54:10
Thy mother is like a vine . . . Ezekiel 19:10
Oh Lord, thou hast searched me . . . Psalms 139:1
Yea, though I walk . . . Psalm 23:4

C H A P T E R   E I G H T :

For we wrestle not against flesh and blood . . . Ephesians 6:12
Shake thyself from the dust . . . Isaiah 52:2

C H A P T E R   N I N E :

Now when the Pharisee . . . Luke 7:39
And Jesus answering . . . Luke 7:40
Tell me therefore . . . Luke 7:42,43
I entered into thy house . . . Luke 7:44–47
Now a certain man was sick . . . John 11:1
The odour of the ointment . . . John 12:3
What I do thou knowest . . . John 13:7,8
Thou shalt never wash my feet . . . John 13:6
Ye call me Master and Lord . . . John 13:13,15
The woman out of whom . . . Mark 16:9
I ascend unto my Father . . . John 20:17
Seemed to them as idle tales . . . Luke 24:11
The other disciple . . . John 20:2

For as yet they knew not . . . John 20:9
Woman, why weepest thou . . . John 20:13–17
With the women . . . Acts 1:14

C H A P T E R   T E N :

The king's daughter is all glorious within . . . Psalms 45:13
Male and female . . . Genesis 1:27
And thou, O tower of the flock . . . Micah 4:8
Before I formed thee in the belly . . . Jeremiah 1:5
Fear thou not . . . Isaiah 41:10
So shall my word be . . . Isaiah 55:11
God is Love . . . I John 4:16
Princes have persecuted . . . Psalm 119:161
For all the law is fulfilled . . . Galatians 5:14
Hast thou entered . . . Job 38:22
Seest thou this woman? . . . Luke 7:44
How fair is thy love . . . Song of Solomon 4:10
Now gather thyself in troops . . . Micah 5:1
They that go down . . . Psalms 107:23
And kings shall be . . . Isaiah 49:23
The Lord recompense . . . Ruth 2:12
And there apperaed a great wonder . . . Revelation 12:1

C H A P T E R   E L E V E N :

In my Father's house . . . John 14:2
She perceiveth . . . Proverbs 31:18

Who can find a virtuous woman? . . . Proverbs 31:10
The heart of her husband . . . Proverbs 31:11–31

C H A P T E R   T W E L V E :

Then she arose . . . Ruth 1:6
And they said unto her . . . Ruth 1:10
If I should have a husband . . . Ruth 1:12–13
Intreat me not to leave thee . . . Ruth 2:1
Where thou diest . . . Ruth 1:17
Is this Naomi? . . . Ruth 1:19
Call Me Not Naomi . . . Ruth 1:20
I went out full . . . Ruth 1:21–22
So Naomi returned . . . Ruth 1:22
And Naomi had a kinsman . . . Ruth 2:1
And Ruth the Moabitess . . . Ruth 2:2
The Lord recompense . . . Ruth 2:12
Before one could know another . . . Ruth 3:14
Go not empty . . . Ruth 3:17
Sit still, my daughter . . . Ruth 3:18
So Boaz took Ruth . . . Ruth 4:13
Blessed be the Lord . . . Ruth 4:14–17
Am I not better than ten sons . . . I Samuel 1:8
O Lord of hosts . . . I Samuel 1:11
How long wilt thou . . . I Samuel 1:14–16
Go in peace . . . I Samuel 1:17
So the woman went her way . . . I Samuel 1:18
Elkanah knew Hannah . . . I Samuel 1:19
Because I asked him of the Lord . . . I Samuel 1:20

C H A P T E R   T H I R T E E N :

Seest thou this woman? . . . Luke 7:44

C H A P T E R   F O U R T E E N :

It was that Mary . . . John 11:2
Martha, Martha . . . Luke 10:41

C H A P T E R   F I F T E E N :

Pastors according . . . Jeremiah 3:15
Which is the way . . . Job 38:19 *Tanakh,* The Holy
Scriptures

C H A P T E R   S I X T E E N :

Wives, submit yourselves . . . Ephesians 5:22
Breathing out threatenings and slaughter . . . Acts 9:1
For the husband . . . Ephesians 5:23
Husbands, love your wives . . . Ephesians 5:25
For this cause . . . Ephesians 5:31–33
Male and female . . . Genesis 1:27
I am the Lord that brought . . . Genesis 15:7
I am the Lord thy God . . . Exodus 20:2

*C H A P T E R
S E V E N T E E N :*

And it came to pass . . . Exodus 16:10

CHAPTER EIGHTEEN

On the day of the Harvest Festival . . . Acts 2:1–3
Is it not yet a very little while . . . Isaiah 29:17
And I saw heaven opened . . . Revelation 19:11
Whom say ye that I am? . . . Matthew 16:15
Upon this rock I will build my church . . . Matthew 16:18
God regardeth not . . . Deuteronomy 10:17
Visit the fatherless and widows . . . James 1:27
Very present help in trouble . . . Psalms 46:1
I do set my bow in the cloud . . . Genesis 9:13,14

CHAPTER NINETEEN:

Thou art highly . . . Luke 1:28
Was troubled at his saying . . . Luke 1:29
With God nothing shall be impossible . . . Luke 1:37
With the moon under her feet . . . Revelation 12:1
Theophilus . . . Luke 1:3
And Simon's wife's mother . . . Luke 4:38
And certain women . . . Luke 8:2
There is none holy as the Lord . . . I Samuel 2:2
The Lord maketh poor . . . I Samuel 2:7
He hath put down . . . Luke 1:52
With God nothing shall be impossible . . . Luke 1:37

C H A P T E R   E I G H T E E N

On the day of the Harvest Festival . . . Acts 2:1–3
Is it not yet a very little while . . . Isaiah 29:17
And I saw heaven opened . . . Revelation 19:11
Whom say ye that I am? . . . Matthew 16:15
Upon this rock I will build my church . . . Matthew 16:18
God regardeth not . . . Deuteronomy 10:17
Visit the fatherless and widows . . . James 1:27
Very present help in trouble . . . Psalms 46:1
I do set my bow in the cloud . . . Genesis 9:13,14

C H A P T E R   N I N E T E E N :

Thou art highly . . . Luke 1:28
Was troubled at his saying . . . Luke 1:29
With God nothing shall be impossible . . . Luke 1:37
With the moon under her feet . . . Revelation 12:1
Theophilus . . . Luke 1:3
And Simon's wife's mother . . . Luke 4:38
And certain women . . . Luke 8:2
There is none holy as the Lord . . . I Samuel 2:2
The Lord maketh poor . . . I Samuel 2:7
He hath put down . . . Luke 1:52
With God nothing shall be impossible . . . Luke 1:37